LURE
ENCYCLOPEDIA

By Frank Prokop

AUSTRALIAN FISHING NETWORK

US Book Shop Distributers
Cardinal Publishers Group
2222 Hillside Avenue
Suite 100
Indianapolis, IN 46218
Tel: (317) 879 0871
Fax: (317) 879 0872
     (317) 846 1557
Toll free: (800) 296 0481
Email: info@cardinalpub.com
Web: www.cardinalpub.com

Published by
Australian Fishing Network
48 Centre Way
Croydon South, Vic. 3136
Australia
Telephone 61 3 9761 4044 Facsimile 61 3 9761 4055
Email: sales@afn.com.au
Website: www.afn.com.au

Photography
Kim Bain
Andy Haan

ISBN 1 86513 076 1

© Frank Prokop, Australian Fishing Network
All rights reserved

First published 2005

CONTENTS

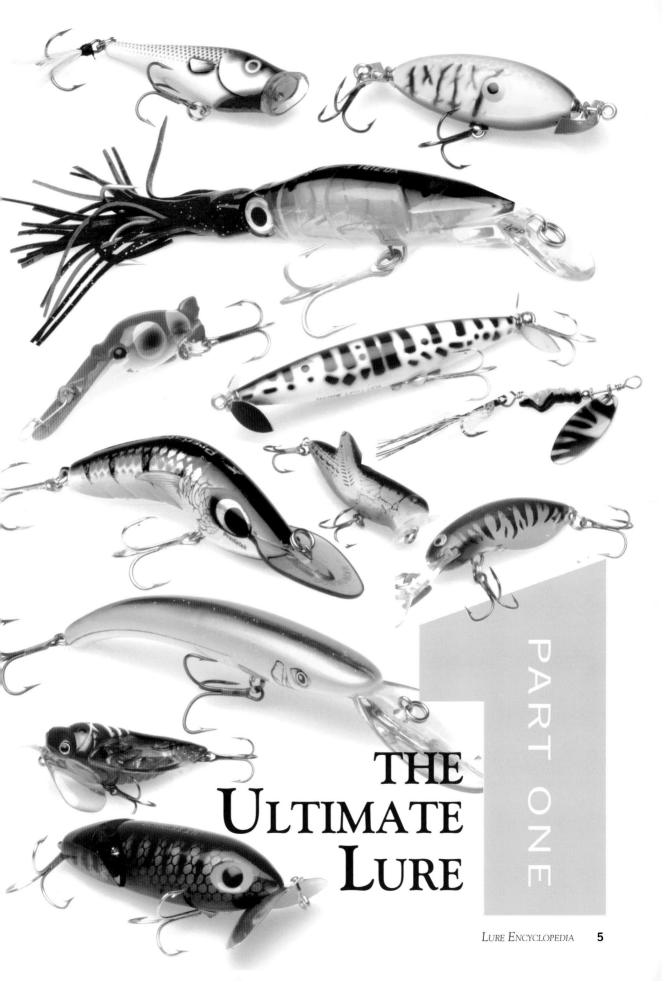

THE
ULTIMATE
LURE

PART ONE

ULTIMATE LURES

Who would think that lumps of plastic, rubber, wood or metal can catch so many different species of fish and increase the enjoyment of fishing for so many people around the United States and the world? Welcome to the exciting and potentially addictive world of lures.

There is a mind-boggling array of lure sizes, colors, weights, styles and prices. Dedication to lure fishing can range from having a spoon or two to having a whole room in the house filled with almost every sample imaginable. Some lures, especially those from granddad's tackle box, if in mint condition are extremely valuable in their own right, as lure collecting rivals collecting fishing reels, antique furniture and stamps as a viable and lucrative hobby.

In the water, the expert can make a suspending lure virtually dance within inches of an only moderately interested fish until it strikes out of hunger, anger or merely to get the annoying thing out of its face. You can select from fizzers, chuggers, paddlers, stick baits and poppers and you haven't even scratched the lure-fishing surface or the surface of the water!

Then there are suspenders, rattlers, and rip baits which could shimmy, roll or wobble on retrieve. Other lures are simpler and are designed to be cast out and wound back in or trolled around at a constant pace. These can act as a great introduction for the novice to experience the delights of lure fishing.

Lure fishing really works! In a number of situations it easily outperforms bait or fly fishing. Lure fishing offers advantages in mobility, variety, skill, and often fight from fish that the angler entices to strike. Lure fishing is cleaner, and leaving a lure in the car is nowhere near as unpleasant a week later as leaving the leftover nightcrawlers behind the back seat.

For many, lure fishing is the method of choice and can be used from crystal clear mountain streams to bluewater fishing for pelagics, and from the surface to depths of more than 100 fathoms. Once an angler starts to get an understanding of some of the techniques, lures can be positively addictive.

This book is the first book specifically designed for the North American market, but represents the fifth comprehensive series of tests of lure performance, characteristics and features, all completed under carefully controlled conditions.

CONDUCTING THESE TESTS

We were able to book the flume tank at a maritime college to conduct the tests. This state-of-the-art tank is used to test the hydrological efficiency of things as diverse as submarines, trawl nets and fishing lures.

As opposed to the previous tests where the lures moved past the test marker, with the flume tank it is the water that

When taking large brown trout from heavily fished streams, depth and size of lure can be extremely important.

The aggressive bluefish likes plenty of flash and some speed to evoke a slashing strike.

moves. The equipment is calibrated so that the water moves at a constant rate. This eliminates any inconsistencies with boat speed between drivers, or even between runs, which was a problem with the previous methodology.

We were also able to eliminate surface drag on the line. The point where the line enters the water while trolling is a point of considerable resistance or drag that can affect the depth of the lure. Eliminating this drag helped to standardize the tests.

Each lure was tied to a test post that was lowered into the tank. For smaller lures, the post was lowered further so that a reading could be obtained and a correction factor was used.

Most importantly, with the flume tank it was possible to directly observe each and every lure as it swam. The action could be much more easily compared with other similar lures. It was also possible to more accurately determine which lures required more or less speed than the standard test speed. These lures were subsequently retested and the optimum depth was included in the final result.

With the very deepest lures the floor of the flume tank acted as a restraint to the diving depth. However, the depth relative to other very deep divers should be pretty accurate.

There is no doubt that lures like the Stretch 25+ and even the Giganticus would well and truly exceed the advertised depths with more line out. Every time I have tested Mann's lures, they have easily exceeded the depth claim. Indeed, many of the shallow divers were running much deeper than

described, indicating how difficult it is to get a crankbait with good action that runs at under three to four feet.

The tables, diagrams, graphs and photographs bear testimony to the scope of the testing. A staggering number of individual tests and measurements were carried out. However, the results do not need to be as daunting as they first appear.

The information allows you to determine a great deal about the performance of your favorite lure to compare it with or select other similar lures if your favorite is not available. You can select a lure to fit a particular fishing situation or change the way you use your favorites when faced with different circumstances when fishing.

RECENT TRENDS IN LURES

Much has changed in the lures scene during the last 10 years or so.

Large companies like Poe's no longer exist, while Storm has joined the Rapala stable and even Rapala themselves have moved their manufacturing from Finland to Ireland. Australian lures have started to have a presence in the American lures scene and have plenty of scope for making converts in the coming years.

Most 'American' lures are now assembled in any of a number of Central American countries such as Mexico, Guatemala and Honduras. Simply put, the labor costs associated with the manufacture and assembly of lures is proving too expensive for domestic labor and it is being outsourced. Mann's remains one of the few true American lure manufacturers.

There has been a profusion of lures produced in Asia in recent times, but these are frequently more generic designs and the evolution of the standard American lure manufacturer does not yet include Southeast Asian manufacture.

There is nothing so spectacular as the attack of a jack crevalle on a surface lure-then things get really interesting with the powerful fight of this fantastic sports fish.

The last ten years has seen enormous changes in the wonderful world of lures.

One major development has been the emergence of high quality suspending lures. A lure that just sits there when the retrieve is stopped has big advantages.

Firstly it lets you work the strike zone very well and very carefully. For ambush predators, the first two to three feet or so of the retrieve is the most vital. This is where the fish has to decide if it wants to eat something before it gets away. While a more quickly moving floater/diver lure may evoke a predatory response in some fish, neutral or passive fish often can't be bothered chasing something. However, if the lure just sits there in front of its face the fish may lazily move over for a bit of a look. When the lure is twitched, the attack response is triggered and the fish simply can't help itself and eats the lure, even if it isn't hungry.

If you have ever watched predatory fish in an aquarium you will understand the principle. A well-fed fish can swim with numbers of small baitfish without incident. But if one of the fish makes a sudden move away from the fish—bang—it gets eaten! The same principle works with lures.

The major downside of the suspending lures is that they do not float backwards from snags, like floating lures do. This means that a lure retriever is more important. There can also be occasions when the pivot back of a floating lure at rest is more attractive than a suspender that just sits there.

Another major development has been that of rippin' minnows. These are lures that actually do very little on a flat retrieve.

An important feature, especially for beginning anglers with spinnerbaits, is that the described weight on the packet is actually for the amount of lead on the hook itself. By the time you add the blades and a skirt, most spinnerbaits actually weigh nearly double the described weight. This is especially important when using small spinnerbaits on light rods meant for smaller lures.

Several interesting lures have come and gone during the period between publications. For example, the Rapala Risto Rap had a life of less than 10 years, although one size has been tested for posterity.

Although not directly related to the lures themselves, braid lines have become standard gear in the last 10 years. They have a smaller diameter than monofilament and no stretch means that an angler can tell the difference between a fish and a snag instantly. Braid lines tangle less, are more resistant to abrasion and easier to use. They are however, quite expensive, must be cut with scissors or a knife, require special knots and the lack of stretch has seen many a brittle carbon fiber rod shatter when loaded too quickly on a fish or snag.

One note about braid however, is that it does have slightly greater resistance in the water for its diameter than monofilament lines. This means that lures will troll slightly shallower for the same diameter line than their monofilament counterparts. Indeed, the resistance of braid lines is the same as for monofilament of about half of their breaking strain rather than their diameter. The 30lb braid ran at about the same depth as 15lb mono and quite a bit shallower than the 7lb (0.2 mm) mono, which was the nearest equivalent diameter tested.

The larger lures were not tested with the 4lb line simply because one of them broke the line during the test, showing that there is a delicate balance between lighter line and effective fishing.

The table shows several important things. One is that the pattern of the tests is remarkably consistent across the different lure types, and that line diameter makes a very big difference in running depths. This effect is more pronounced with smaller lures or those with smaller bibs where the resistance of the line will have a greater effect on depth and also on action.

Line diameter comparison – at standard speed of 2 knots

No.	Lure	Cord 0.73 mm	18lb, 0.35 mm mono	Book Result @ 22ft	30lb Fins Braid 8lb diam.	20lb Fins Braid 6lb diam.	Asso Mono 14lb, 0.3 mm	Asso Mono 12lb, 0.28 mm	Asso Mono 7lb, 0.2 mm	Asso Mono 4lb, 0.16 mm	Book Result for 66ft
228	Burmek B1 Pike Jointed	3'	3' 1"	3' 4"	2' 10"	3' 4"	3' 4"	3' 4"	3' 5"		8' 3"
230	Predatek MicroMin Shallow	3' 1"	3' 7"	3' 5"	3' 11"	4' 1"	4' 3"	4' 5"	4' 11"	5' 3"	8' 6"
350	Rapala Shad Rap Jointed JSR5	3' 5"	4' 5"	4' 7"	4' 5"	4' 11"	5' 1"	5' 1"	5' 7"	5' 11"	12' 3"
387	StumpJumper 2 Shallow bib	4' 3"	5' 3"	5' 1"	5' 5"	5' 7"	5' 3"	5' 7"	5' 5"	5' 11"	13' 9"
400	Yo-Zuri Hydro Squirt	4' 3"	5' 3"	5' 5"	5' 1"	5' 5"	5' 9"	5' 9"	6' 3"		14' 6"
409	Rapala Magnum CD-11	3' 7"	4' 10"	4' 11"	4' 7"	5' 3"	5' 3"	5' 9"	6' 3"		14' 9"
441	Predatek Boomerang 65	5' 5"	6' 1"	6' 1"	5' 11"	6' 3"	6' 3"	6' 5"	6' 11"		16' 3"
444	DK Lures Scale Raza 20+	5' 7"	6' 1"	5' 11"	5' 9"	6' 1"	6' 7"	6' 8"	7'	7' 5"	16' 6"
460	Nilsmaster Jumbo DD	5' 5"	5' 11"	5' 11"	5' 9"	5' 11"	6' 3"	6' 3"	6' 8"		17' 6"
471	Hellbender - Magnum	5' 7"	6' 3"	6' 3"	6' 1"	6' 3"	6' 5"	6' 8"	6' 11"		18' 6"
492	Newell Kadaitcha	6' 3"	6' 8"	6' 8"	6' 7"	6' 7"	7' 2"	7' 2"	7' 5"		22' 6"
495	Halco RMG Scorpion 150 XDD	6' 5"	6' 8"	6' 7"	6' 11"	7'	7' 2"	7' 5"	7' 6"		23'

RESULTS

It was fascinating to be able to watch the best and most successful lures in the world swimming before your eyes in the flume tank. One after the other they came—clip, swim, adjust depth of the tow post, video, record results, give the all clear and wait for the next lure. Hour after hour they came.

For days we recorded the results while the team at the top of the tank got lures from their specially numbered bags, clipped them on and lowered them into the water, hauled them in and put the lure into the box ready to be sorted for the photographs which appear in the book.

And then it was to the computer room to tabulate, analyze and format the results so that they can be presented.

Each and every time we undertake these tests there are a few surprises in the results. And for this, the largest test series, there were a fair share of somewhat surprising results. I will leave it to the discerning reader to pore through the test results to determine which results do not seem to fit exactly, but stress that this, while a scientific test under controlled conditions, is not the absolute answer to all questions. I wish those who try for this perfection in later tests all the very best.

The walleye is highly prized and, depending upon the time of year, can be aggressive or passive, but rewards the patient and careful angler.

RUNDOWN ON RESULTS

It was great to be able to include the variety of surface lures in this book. There are many saltwater and freshwater species that really adore surface lures. There are a variety of action types that can be fished really fast (saltwater poppers), to medium retrieve (some paddlers and fizzers) to really, really slow (stick baits among others). As technology improves, the incredibly life-like River2Sea Cicada Pop is competing with the old faithful Jitterbug and Crazy Crawler.

For this set of tests, there were many chrome or metal lures. These lures are cheap and successful. They are applicable to many situations, ranging from trout to tuna and most species in between. Metal lures either run quite shallow and are particularly effective for active or pelagic species, or are used for deep vertical jigging.

I am a big fan of wooden lures. Apart from the fact that wooden lures form the backbone of the increasing lure-collecting market, they also require greater attention to detail and therefore have greater individuality. They have a special appeal that the plastic lures cannot match. I know this is a personal preference, but I feel better using wooden lures.

Plastic lures make up the majority of crankbaits including the majority of the very best lures and the number one lure from the tests. They can include rattles and even special counterbalancing chambers. The quality controls can be much better overall, but if a mould spreads, these lures can be difficult to tune.

Plastic lures also suffer as a group in that some Asian imitations are of dubious quality. A few of the Chinese specials looked fantastic but were unable to be tuned due to design faults. However, other lures from this category, such as the Producers lures represent excellent value for money and are almost always dependable. Note that if you pay less, you cannot expect perfection every time and you will have to learn to tune many of these lures to make them run straight.

THE DEEPEST DOZEN

The deepest dozen presents a range of very deep diving lures with real fresh and saltwater applications, although you would need specialized tackle to use the Giganticus from Mann's on a regular basis. Putting on a lure with a retail price of around $250 also requires faith in the equipment being able to bring both lure and fish back to the boat.

There are three Australian lures in the deepest dozen, with the difficult to obtain but fantastic Kadaitcha, the RMG Scorpion 150XDD and the Predatek Boomerang Ultra-Deep 80 running deepest.

The other representatives include household names such as Rapala, Bomber, Storm, Luhr Jensen and especially Mann's.

These lures can cover most deep diving fresh and saltwater applications. They provide flexibility with crash dive casting depths (for the majority). You can also troll these lures up short for maximum maneuverability around saltwater reefs, drowned hilltops or deep cover or troll the back of the prop wash which is frequently overlooked by anglers who insist on trolling with 50–100 yards of line behind the boat.

It is important to point out that a lure that runs deepest may not catch most or even many fish. You need to put your lure in places where it is most likely to get eaten. Active fish will readily move upwards to take a lure but even they rarely move downwards, so you may well be trolling below the fish.

Absolute depth can be very important, especially for some species, but it should not be the only attribute of a lure.

WHAT MAKES A GOOD LURE?

Using lures is fun. Casting and trolling them everywhere from bluewater for gamefish, through mangrove creeks, inshore reefs, rocks and estuaries to alpine rivers, lakes, slower rivers in the tropics and cooler waters can be the most successful and satisfying way to fish in many situations. It is simply a matter of tying on a lure, chucking it out and either retrieving it or letting it swim behind the boat while you cruise around. Right?—Wrong! Very wrong.

There is a whole lot more to fishing with lures, although the random casting from the local dock often has terrific fun catching the odd aggressive fish. But if you want to improve your catches and meet the challenge of successful lure fishing and enjoy it more, then here is a whole host of hints and information for you to digest and try.

Most anglers have definite ideas about what constitutes a good lure. Usually their favorite lure is determined by a history of success. This success generally develops on the basis of 'fish' talk, what the fishing magazines say is hot, what your buddies are using, local knowledge and what your recent results have been.

The adage that you can only use lures one at a time is certainly true and most anglers, resplendent with bulging tackle boxes containing hundreds of the latest lure offerings, will continue to drag the same two or three around for hour after hour, even when getting no hits whatsoever. Consequently, favorite lures will always catch more fish than those that slowly rust in the bottom of the tackle box.

Let's assume that we were going to start selecting lures based upon their quality, special features and versatility. What factors are important in selecting the best lures? To be objective, we will ignore the rumor that a mysterious individual caught heaps on his own special 'one-off' lure last week.

Some of the most important considerations for purchasing lures are the finish, price, action, size, and availability.

The finish gives a good indication of how the lure will perform when you are using it. Splotchy paint work, crooked bibs and poor sanding on wooden lures or rough joins, bubbled finishes and glue globs on plastic lures gives an indication that something else is probably not right. If you have several examples of one lure type, all of which are difficult to tune, forget them. Often the hooks or hook attachments are of inferior quality and may give out on that trophy fish.

It's an advantage if the lure is available in a variety of sizes. This will allow you to change size without altering other lure characteristics. This is important when targeting different species and sizes of fish and imitating different sizes of prey. Lures with wider ranges have an edge in this area.

In looking for the perfect lure, we give you the thoughts of long time Australian lure making master Steve Kovacs of Custom Crafted lures. Nothing has changed since 1991, when Steve first gave me this insight, to make this comment

THE TOP LURES FROM AN ACTIO

No.	Lure	Depth @ 66 ft	Action	Manufacturer
66	Wobbler 10 g Sparkler	1'	Medium wobble	Halco
94	Inkoo 26 g	2' 9"	Medium wobble	Blue Fox
106	Jointed Swim Whizz	3'	Wide sway, wide roll	Homer Le Blanc
110	Salty Tasmanian Devil	3' 6"	Wide wobble, wide pitch	Wigston's
141	Husky Jerk HJ8	5'	Tight roll, medium pitch	Rapala
165	Tasmanian Devil Dual Depth	6'	Wide wobble	Wigston's
188	Hot Shot 60	7' 3"	Medium sway	Luhr Jensen
195	Master Shad	7' 6"	Very wide sway, medium pitch	Bagley
205	Shad Rap Jointed JSR4	7' 9"	Medium sway	Rapala
221	Shallow Thunder 15	8'	Medium sway, medium roll	Storm
225	Mini Z Shallow	8' 3"	Tight roll, tight pitch	The Producers
228	Burmek B1 Pike Jointed	8' 3"	Medium sway	Uncle Josh
235	Shakespeare Minnow	8' 6"	Medium sway, medium roll	Shakespeare Lures
266	Spence Scout	9' 3"	Tight sway	Strike King Lure Co.
274	Super Spot	9' 9"	Tight sway, vibrate	Cotton Cordell
289	MinMin Deep	10'	Tight sway	Predatek
294	Honey B	10' 6"	Tight sway	Bagley
297	TD Hyper Shad Ti60	10' 6"	Medium sway	Team Daiwa
315	Stretch 5+	11' 3"	Tight sway	Mann's Lures
334	Tail Dancer TD9	11' 9"	Medium sway, medium roll	Rapala
335	Sliver Jointed 13	11' 9"	Tight sway, medium roll	Rapala
350	Shad Rap Jointed JSR5	12' 3"	Fast sway, tight pitch	Rapala
352	Super Shad Rap 14	12' 6"	Tight sway, medium roll	Rapala
377	Invincible 25	13' 6"	Medium roll	Nilsmaster
381	Wiggle Wart	13' 6"	Medium sway	Storm
382	Deep Crawfish	13' 6"	Tight sway	Rebel
384	Bevy Shad 75	13' 6"	Tight sway, tight roll	Lucky Craft Lures
393	Bunyip	14'	Medium wide sway	Predatek
400	Hydro Squirt	14' 6"	Medium wobble, tight roll	Yo-Zuri Lures
403	Bandit 400 Series	14' 6"	Medium sway, medium pitch	Bandit Lures

any less relevant to lure manufacturers or users of today and tomorrow.

There are a lot of novice fishermen around so one of the most important features is to design a lure that will track true and maintain a good depth at a variety of trolling speeds. Many anglers, both experienced and new, cannot, or do not know how to tune a lure and aren't interested in learning! If the lure maker can design a lure that is very easy to tune and rarely plays up then he is well in front of his competitors. Rattles or not, sinking or floating, size of bib, location of pull point, angle and shape of bib, size of lure including size of hooks, action required etc, etc, etc. All are thoughts and considerations that race through a dedicated lure maker's mind each time a new lure is created and there is always another design on the backburner.

Our tests provided us with the perfect forum to see if the perfect lure has been created. The verdict—there is always room for improvement, and we will still most likely tie on our favorite lure first.

THE BEST LURES

Action is by far one of the most important key attributes of a good lure. Key actions include a tight sway, wobble or vibrating action for trout and a medium or wide sway for native fish. Metal lures and poppers are particularly successful for the pelagic marine species.

There are basically three directions which a lure can move in while being trolled or retrieved. With the action description these are described as sway (side to side action), wobble (rolling action) and pitch (bucking up and down action).

There are very few lures that can move in all three directions without losing control and threatening to blow out. A lure traveling at the right speed will sway and wobble. It may occasionally dart out from side to side, which is particularly enticing to fish. As the speed increases, these darts to the side become wider and the recovery of the lure becomes more difficult. Finally the lure 'blows out' and rolls over onto its back and planes to the surface.

Few lures have the capacity to also move in the third direction—which is pitch. In most instances, once a lure starts 'bucking', it is likely to blow out at any increase in speed. With most lures, once they started to increase their pitch (bucking), they needed to be run more slowly and then they performed better. It can be a very fine line between great erratic action and a lure that is deemed unreliable because it is too fussy with its speed and keeps coming to the surface.

The assessment of action and quality is somewhat subjective. What looks attractive to us standing outside the flume tank might not look nearly as attractive to the fish.

However, after testing 1065 lures, I am willing to go out on a limb and nominate the 'Best' lure in the tests. It is the Australian-made **DK Lures Scale Raza 20+**. The Yo-Zuri Hydro Squirt, Rapala Jointed Shad Rap 5, Reef Runner Deep Diver, Kadaitcha, MinMin Deep and Magnum Hellbender were also deemed to be exceptional lures.

THE ATTRACTIVE QUALITIES IN A LURE—THE 'SO DAM HOT' FORMULA

Since most lures are supposed to imitate food or stimulate an aggressive response in fish, it is necessary to look at the important factors that

ERSPECTIVE—RANKED BY DEPTH

No.	Lure	Depth @ 66 ft	Action	Manufacturer
405	Hot Lips Express 1/4oz	14' 6"	Medium sway	Luhr Jensen
406	Combat	14' 9"	Medium sway	Halco
409	Magnum CD-11	14' 9"	Medium sway	Rapala
416	Invincible DR 12 cm	15'	Medium sway, medium pitch	Nilsmaster
418	Magnum wiggle wart (US made)	15' 3"	Medium sway, tight pitch	Storm
421	Deep Wart	15' 6"	Medium sway	Storm
424	Probe	15' 6"	Medium sway, tight pitch	Rabble Rouser Lures
427	Wiggle Wart	15' 9"	Medium sway	Storm
431	Viper 150	16'	Tight sway, tight roll	Predatek
436	Deep Z	16'	Tight sway, tight pitch	The Producers
437	Invincible DR15	16'	Medium roll	Nilsmaster
438	Deep ThunderStick	16'	Medium sway, tight roll	Storm
441	Boomerang 65	16' 3"	Tight sway, medium pitch	Predatek
443	Magnum CD-9	16' 6"	Tight sway	Rapala
444	Scale Raza 20+	16' 6"	Medium sway, tight pitch	DK Lures
445	Spoonbill	16' 6"	Medium sway, medium roll	Predatek
454	Double Downer #3	17'	Medium sway	The Producers
460	Jumbo DD	17' 6"	Medium sway, medium pitch	Nilsmaster
468	Heavy Duty Stretch 12+	18' 3"	Tight sway	Mann's Lures
471	Hellbender - Magnum	18' 6"	Medium wide sway	Pradco Lures
472	Prime DD Crankbait 25	18' 9"	Medium sway, tight roll	Spro
480	Hot'N Tot Magnum (old)	19' 9"	Medium sway	Storm
481	Stumpjumper 1 deep bib	20'	Medium wide sway	JJ's Lures
483	TD Hyper Crank Ti65	20'	Wide sway	Team Diawa
487	Reef Runner Deep Diver	21	Wide sway	Reef Runner Tackle Co.
488	Hydro Magnum 95 g	21'	Slow medium sway	Yo-Zuri Lures
492	Kadaitcha	22' 6"	Wide sway	Peter Newell Lures
493	Long A H-Duty	22' 6"	Wide sway	Bomber
495	RMG Scorpion 150 XDD Crazy Deep	23'	Wide sway, tight roll	Halco
500	Hot Lips Express 3/4oz	25'	Wide sway	Luhr Jensen

put a fish on your line.

This simple formula can help novice anglers to improve their capacity to catch a few fish when no one else is catching much at all. The importance of angler-controlled factors such as experience and flexibility, which make an enormous difference to results, can only be gained through hours on the water, but that's not such a bad punishment is it?

The crucial factors in order are:
1. Skill (Knowledge)
2. Objectivity (Flexibility)
3. Depth
4. Action
5. Mass (Size)
6. Haste (Speed)
7. Outline (Shape)
8. Tone (Color)

This gives <u>SO DAM HOT</u>- The formula for the successful use of lures.

SKILL

Knowledge, skill and experience are extremely important attributes for the successful use of lures. They are independent of the lures themselves and need to be gathered yourself or learned from watching or fishing with someone who knows what works best.

While books like this and fishing magazines provide wonderful tips and hints to make you more successful, there is no substitute for getting out there and having a go yourself. It is only when you start getting hits on casts that land right next to the snag for bass or crappies that you can see just how important it is. And with practice and good equipment, putting the lures into the right spot more often means that your catches will improve. Those without a lot of experience will catch fish, but those with it will catch them much more consistently.

OBJECTIVITY (FLEXIBILITY)

Some anglers have one or two tried and true lures or techniques and will stick with them through thick and thin. These old favorites have consistently performed and as a consequence get a swim most often. This is fine when things are going well, but I firmly believe that the truly great anglers are not the ones who catch 12 when everyone else is catching 6 or 7 fish, but the angler that catches one or two when everyone else is coming back empty handed.

It is really important to be open-minded and keep trying new things and not just as a last resort. Try a larger lure or a smaller one, use a suspending lure instead of a floater or give a spinnerbait or rattlin' spot lure a go. If you are getting follows but not hits, experiment until you get the right combination that turns a day of frustration into a day to remember.

DEPTH

Successful anglers are those who keep their lures in areas where they can be eaten by the most fish for the longest possible time. The strike zone is three-dimensional and although fish will move upwards more readily than they will

move downwards to take a lure, you need to get the lure close enough to the fish to evoke a response.

Most fish are lazy. They want to get the best possible return in food for expending the least possible energy. If your lure is right in front of their nose you will get many more hits than if they have to move up 15 feet in the water column (which is about equivalent to about one atmosphere of pressure).

Put in its simplest terms, it is no good trolling for trout at one yard deep when the surface temperature is 60 degree, or trolling with downriggers if specimens you are fishing for are rising all around you.

In practice, the use of depth can dramatically improve your lure-fishing results. Presenting your lure (or bait if you are using more active methods) where target fish can take it, must, logic dictates, improve your results.

ACTION AND MASS

Action and mass (size) can be varied regularly with different lures trolled at the same time—such as a Rapala Fat Rap, a Spinnerbait and a Flatfish. It is possible to quickly confirm which size and action type is working best, and alter the other lures to further explore these areas.

Some action types work better for some species and it pays to match the hatch in terms of what the fish are eating to maximize strikes.

Better use of things such as trolling sinkers, different trolling lengths, lighter or heavier line or braid lines will enable you to present a much wider variety of lures at the same depth. If your sounder is telling you that fish are there, you should experiment to see if you can catch them.

HASTE (SPEED)

Speed (haste) is more difficult to experiment with and often needs a complete change of lure type. As a result, anglers do not change speeds too often whilst fishing.

For example, lures such as the Flatfish and Tasmanian Devil are incompatible when trolling. You either troll with medium paced lures such as the Rapala Countdown minnows, other spoons or a Tasmanian Devil, or with slow running lures to use with a Flatfish, Mann's, or Hot Shot.

This is an area worth investigating if other tactics are not working.

OUTLINE (SHAPE)

I have included outline (shape or profile) because there are times when it makes a dramatic difference. In fresh water, many baitfish are long and skinny. Lures like the Rapala minnows are excellent imitations and do very well. In salt water, baitfish and shrimp also have a narrow profile and many metal and crankbait lures imitate these common foods.

However, other species such as goldfish and alwifes are more bulky, so lures with a wider profile can work better. Crawfish provide yet another outline that can be imitated. In salt water, many juvenile fish have a broader profile.

In low light conditions or murky water, the general profile of your lure or their prey would be all that would register with a fish. A quick inspection of the stomach contents of your first fish should provide a short-cut to the size and profile departments

TONE (COLOR)

Lastly there is color (tone). It is truly said that color catches more fishermen than fish. I am not suggesting that color is irrelevant, but to change color ten times before experimenting with the other factors is not making best use of your fishing time.

In the flume tank, the contrast of light and dark colors showed up extremely well under water. The classical coachdog or striped patterns were far more visible than single color lures. Even the stripes on a Fat Rap perch color, which are difficult to see out of water, were very obvious in the tank. The new holographic colors and metallic finishes did add extra flash and have an important place.

With some of the Chinese lures, fantastic colors can mask ordinary action and performance; so don't just fall for a pretty face with a lure.

It is interesting to note that red lures are much more popular than black ones, yet at a trolling depth of 15 feet, the red washes out completely. Therefore, in a fishing sense, red is, and has been for a long time the 'new' black. Conversely, purple maintains its color at depth and has a dark outline with some color evident, which makes this a popular choice for deep situations and low light conditions.

Research has shown that fluorescent colors are a definite turn on for some species at some times while they can be a turn off at other times. Color is one area where fishes' underwater perception may be vastly different to ours, but in my experience, the times when only one color works effectively are far fewer than the tales in bars would have you believe.

At the end of the day, changing colors increases confidence and improves the way we fish. This, and a tendency to need to own every lure in every color, not only helps the economy, it adds to the overall enjoyment of lure fishing.

LURE FISHING TACTICS

All this information is of only passing interest if it can't be put into practical use. The lure depths are much easier to use if you have a good quality depth sounder.

If the sounder is able to identify where the fish are, it is a matter of presenting a lure that will have the right action and run at the right depth. This is where these tables come into their own.

Many of us are guilty of trolling past a fish on the sounder and shaking our heads if we don't get a strike. Comments like 'Probably a trash fish' or 'school of baitfish', often follow. We ignore the fact that last week those same blips were good fish that were taking lures.

Although depth is perhaps the most critical element in successful trolling, it needs to be considered as only part of the overall SO DAM HOT picture.

With many cover-orientated species, locating a fish is only the beginning of the battle. With perseverance, and the patience to experiment until a successful formula is reached, many of these fish can be coaxed into striking.

When spawning, salmon require a lure with plenty of flash or colour to evoke a predatory rather than a feeding response. The reward can be a fish of a lifetime.

ACTIVE NEUTRAL AND PASSIVE FISH

Fish can be loosely grouped into active, neutral and passive in their behavior.

How they react to your lure will be determined by a variety of factors relating to the weather, season, availability of food and your presentation.

Contrary to local belief, it is very rare that fish aren't hungry. They are all designed to feed well while food is plentiful and this helps growth or the development of eggs or sperm. Some species will develop thick bands of fat if they remain where food is plentiful, while bluefish simply regurgitate their food to keep feeding.

ACTIVE FISH

Active or aggressive fish are the stuff of fishing dreams. This is when trout and bass hit anything you put in front of them and even fish like muskies seem to chase lures anywhere.

At times when fish are particularly active, the main objective is to put a lure close enough for the fish to see and eat it. Active fish will often move great distances to catch food, especially at their preferred depth.

It is possible to fish too deep at these times and this can be a big risk. Active fish will readily move up to take a lure, but will rarely move deeper. It is therefore possible to be dragging your lure through a fish desert even though you could be only slightly too deep.

Slab sized crappies can be taken with crankbaits presented to standing timber or weed edges.

Catching active fish is well illustrated when flatlining spoons or lures like the Tasmanian Devil in fresh water. They run shallowly, but give off strong vibrations, are highly visible and attract active, feeding trout like magnets.

The factors which trigger large numbers of fish to become active include a rising water level or low level floods, rising barometer (although local storms often make some species very active), pre- spawning or post- spawning behavior, moon phases and the availability of preferred food items (e.g. insect hatches, crawfish, baitfish schools or drowned worms). Spawning aggregations in particular can make fish very aggressive, either because the competition for available food is intense or as part of protecting their areas from other fish.

NEUTRAL FISH

Neutral fish are still catchable but require a better presentation. Factors such as lure size and action may mean the difference between success and failure.

Many fish, and especially ambush feeders, spend a great deal of their time in a neutral mode. They will feed when the right food presents itself, but they will not expend a lot of energy in catching it. They may move a few feet to hit a lure, but they may just nudge it, or swipe and miss.

When there are large numbers of neutral fish, you have to work at it. But your efforts will be rewarded. Experiments pay off and what works for one lake, bay or even fish may not be the answer around the corner.

With trout, additional attractors such as Ford Fenders or

dodgers are often the trigger that induces strikes. Sometimes fluorescent colors help, but your lure needs to be closer to the fish to get a strike.

Conditions that result in neutral fish include constant or slowly falling water levels, long term stable barometer, continuing clear or foul weather and an over-abundance of food.

PASSIVE FISH

Passive or inactive fish present a real challenge. This is when the tough get going and only the best anglers can consistently take fish.

There is no doubt that there is an element of luck, as finding the one active fish on a day when everything else is holed up can be the only fish taken. However, to consistently take fish under these circumstances takes real skill and perseverance.

Presentations can be perfect and still not get a response. You can often drag a lure past the nose of a passive brown trout or red drum forever without ever getting a response. However, many species will reward persistence and will often get sick of a lure if you don't get tired of putting it in front of them first.

Conditions that turn fish off include falling water levels, falling barometer, unsuitable water, pH or oxygen levels and actual spawning.

TACTICS FOR ADVERSE CONDITIONS

Even in the most adverse conditions there will still be the odd neutral or active fish, so a mobile approach often works.

Dams or estuaries, which have had strong winds for several days, are good examples. This frequently means that the usual tactics produce little more than a wet and uncomfortable day. Most anglers head for the lee shore and a bit of peace. Wrong!

A much better tactic is to cast or troll the windward shore. Often there is a well-defined line of muddy water where the waves have disturbed the shore. That mud is full of food that is either eaten by predators or attracts forage fish. Fish the current line just like you would out at sea.

Adverse conditions can often be used to advantage with a careful plan of attack.

ACHIEVING MAXIMUM DEPTH

There is a perception that you can let out unlimited amounts of line to get a lure to run deeper. This is not the case.

There is a point at which the drag on the line through the water is greater than the diving ability of the lure's bib and the lure will actually run shallower with more line out. There is an optimum drop back for all lures: for deep divers it is generally around 70 feet, and with trout lures it is around 100 feet, which is why we did our tests at these distances.

Speed, too, is important. If you get above or below the optimum speed listed in the chart, the lure action changes, often resulting in below par performance. Another disadvantage of trolling with long lines is the enormous stretch in monofilament line (if you are using it) that reduces your hook-setting ability. You are also very restricted in your ability to **maneuver**, especially if there are several lines out at once, or you are trolling in close around cover.

As a result I generally prefer to troll a deeper running lure on a shorter line to achieve the same depth, even in most saltwater trolling situations. This means that I have good contact with the lure; I can troll a lot tighter to the shore or have greater control in or near the wake and hopefully keep the lure in the strike zone for longer.

There is some variability in the diving ability of the tested lures. Some lures such as the Magnum Hellbender are renowned for their 'crash dive' capability, while many of the medium diving lures do not dive much deeper on a longer cast or with more line out on the troll.

TRYING DIFFERENT DEPTHS

Fishing can be more difficult if fish are showing at a variety of depths. It pays to keep in mind that the fish may be more active at one level than another.

Trout can demonstrate this. Frequently, large numbers will show on the sounder near the thermocline with the odd fish near the surface. Concentrating on the deep fish can be a waste of time as the surface fish are often actively feeding and able to be caught more easily.

Because the effectiveness of specific lures can vary from day to day, try to cover your options quickly. I will always accept a partner's strike as incidental, but if they pick up two hits in a row, l want to know what I'm doing wrong.

CASTING WITH DIVING LURES

There is at least as much speculation about the performance of diving lures when cast and retrieved as there is about their trolling depth. The classical floating diving lure has a lot of faults when it comes to many casting situations.

It is well known that with many species such as bass, your cast should land within a foot or so of the cover. If you are further out you can usually forget about it. This leaves an effective strike zone of much less than three feet.

Because of the constraints of the flume tank, we were not able to run any further casting tests. However, we have run a variety of casting tests during previous lures' tests. As a rough guide, you can use the trolling depth to get an idea of the performance of the tested lures when cast and retrieved.

The average deep diving lure only reaches about 25 percent of its running depth (66 feet of line) after 5 feet of the retrieve. For a lure that trolls at 12 feet, it will be only 3 feet deep at this point.

For a fish near the bottom of a snag in 12 foot of water, the fish will have to move nearly the full 12 feet to eat your lure if you merely cast straight to the snag. This distance is much further with shallow diving lures like the floating Rapala series.

This information is very interesting, because although a lure that trolls at 12 feet gets down three feet deep after 5 foot of the retrieve, it takes another 15 feet of winding to get down to 6 feet. The fish has to move a hell of a long way to eat it and it is only active fish that are really chasing these lures.

Generally, most lures reach about 33 percent (one third)

of the listed trolling depth (on 66 feet of line) after 10 foot of the retrieve. This goes down to around 45 percent after 20 foot and approximately 50–60 percent after 30 feet.

There is considerable variation in the maximum depth reached by lures on the retrieve. This is difficult to test due to the variability of casting performance of each lure. While fishing, wind, angler ability and different spool levels vary the cast distance, and hence the maximum depth that a lure could reach on any given cast.

But it is really the critical part of the cast, where it is closest to fish-holding cover that is important. For many cover-associated fish, this is at the beginning of the cast. With ambush feeders this critical part of the cast could be where the lure comes up over a drop-off onto shallows.

The maximum cast depth varied from 50 percent to nearly 90 percent of the trolled depth. A very rough average was around 75 percent. This means that a lure which trolls at 12 foot deep should get down to around 9 foot 6 inches or so on a long cast and this depth is achieved at around 75 percent of the distance retrieved.

CASTING TACTICS

It can be very difficult to catch passive fish with a standard cast and retrieve. Most lures are going so far over their heads that they won't even bother the fish. There are two changes of tactic that work very well in these circumstances. The first is to change the angle of attack.

If possible, cast well beyond the place where you think the fish is. This will put the lure much deeper when it passes. If

One of the world's most prized sports fish, the peacock bass, can attack a shallow running crankbait with ferocity.

the fish doesn't have to move so far, more fish will be inclined to strike.

You should use far more parallel casts. Instead of just casting directly at the fish-holding cover all the time, make your casts along it. This gets the lure closer to where the fish are most likely to be. This is also highly successful when fish are patrolling the outer edges of weed beds or reefs. Placing a cast where the lure stays in 'fishy' looking water for the longest possible time will, in the long run, increase your fishing success.

There are also times when it pays to cast out from shore, even if you have a boat. Always try to work the shore, casting the lure so that it is at the right depth at the right place.

Another tactic is to use a sinking lure. In this way, your retrieve can begin right in the strike zone. Hits are often hard and after only one or two cranks of the handle.

This is one of the reasons why jigs, spinnerbaits and plastic worms are so successful for so many species. These lures are presented where they can be eaten with the minimum amount of energy wasted.

Spoons, rattlin' spot lures and spinnerbaits are relatively cheap and do the job on a wide range of species very well. They sink right next to cover and can start the retrieve right on a fish's nose that is sitting at the bottom of a snag or ledge. Many other lures are slow sinkers and can drift slowly down a rocky ledge or next to drowned timber. I know that it is expensive to lose sinking lures like some of the Bagley's and Rapala Countdowns, but they work very well. You can even add a split shot to the line or Storm suspend dot to the lure to make a floating lure into a slow sinker. However, the action will be slightly different with this 'doctoring'.

Another thing to bear in mind when casting is the way the lure finishes the retrieve. Most diving lures continue to dive, though at a slower rate, until they are nearly back to the rod. Some lures such as the Fat Raps and Hellbenders actually go under the boat before turning around as they rise to the surface.

With species such as pike, you will get lots of hits at the point where the lure stops diving and starts to come back up to the surface. With a bit of practice you can feel that the lure changes its beat at this point. Use one of the best tricks going—pause.

A pause of as little as half a second when the lure starts to plane upwards will greatly increase the number of strikes you will get. I have watched many different species for many hours in fish tanks while working on research projects. They will swim up to a baitfish to watch it and even nudge it with their nose. The instant the fish makes a move to escape it is gulped down.

By pausing, many marine ambush feeders swim up to see what is going on. When the retrieve is started again, instinct takes over and they have already eaten your lure whether they really wanted it or not. This trick also works if you can feel a fish nudging or bumping your lure during the retrieve. A slight pause often gets a hookup.

Northern pike, in particular, often follow lures up to the surface. They can even stick their heads out of the water trying unsuccessfully to eat a lure. Make sure you leave a couple of feet of line off the rod tip when you finish each cast. If you get a follow, stick your rod under the water and make an exaggerated figure of eight. Keep your drag light and hang on, because the strikes are dramatic and the fight memorable at such close quarters. Other species like barracuda and some crevalle will also hit frequently in this way.

CONCLUSIONS

There is much more to lure fishing than just tying on a lure and chucking and winding. By using the information in this book, you should be able to better select what fish to target and where to make your cast. You should be better able to select a lure to do the job and know what it will be doing when you are casting or trolling with different lines or distances behind the boat.

And you should be able to select new lures that give you new features, depths, actions or other attributes to cover a wider range of situations while you are fishing.

When you have caught your first fish with lures your addiction will increase. And with your 100,000[th] fish you will continue to experience the excitement and thrill of catching fish on lures.

Good luck with your fishing. Take a kid fishing and help to keep our aquatic environment clean and healthy for the next generation.

It isn't just Australian lures that are doing well in North America. Aussie export Kim Bain has been making a name for herself with impressive performances on the pro bass tour.

THE
TEST
RESULTS

PART TWO

NUMBER	LURE	DEPTH (FT) ON 66 FT	MAKER'S STATED DEPTH	ACTION	COMMENTS	FLOATING – SINKING – SUSPENDING	BODY MATERIAL PLASTIC – METAL – WOOD – RUBBER	BIB MATERIAL	WIDTH OF BIB (in)	TOW POINT	ACTUAL WEIGHT (oz)	ACTUAL BODY LENGTH (in)	LENGTH WITH BIB (in)
1	Hawg Stopper #1 F	0	Surface	Chugger	Value for money	F	P	Bibless	0.89	Nose	$5/16$	$1^1/2$	$2^1/4$
2	Hopper Popper HP04	0	Surface	Chugger	Very realistic finish	F	P	Bibless	0.36	Nose	$1/16$	$1^5/8$	$1^3/4$
3	Crickhopper PopR	0	Surface	Chugger	Works at different speeds	F	P	Bibless	0.65	Nose	$1/8$	$1^3/4$	$2^1/8$
4	Hula Popper	0	Surface	Chugger	An all time classic	F	P	Bibless	0.86	Nose	$3/8$	$1^7/8$	$2^3/8$
5	Teeny Pop R	0	Surface	Chugger	Strong bloop on retrieve	F	P	Bibless	0.50	Nose	$1/8$	$1^7/8$	2
6	Popper 5/8oz F	0	Surface	Chugger	Long tail	F	P	Bibless	0.75	Nose	$3/8$	$2^1/4$	$2^1/2$
7	Skitter Pop SP-5	0	Surface	Chugger	High quality lure	F	W	Bibless	0.47	Nose	$1/4$	$2^1/4$	$2^1/2$
8	Chug Bug 6 cm	0	Surface	Chugger	Slender profile can work like stick bait	F	P	Bibless	0.58	Nose	$1/4$	$2^3/8$	$2^5/8$
9	Pop-R Excalibur	0	Surface	Chugger	Oldie but goodie	F	P	Bibless	0.73	Nose	$3/8$	$2^1/2$	3
10	Bubble Pop 65	0	Surface	Chugger	Can work at fast retrieve	F	P	Bibless	0.61	Nose	$1/4$	$2^1/2$	$2^3/4$
11	Frenzy Surface	0	Surface	Chugger	Strong following this lure	F	P	Bibless	0.57	Nose	$5/16$	$2^5/8$	$2^7/8$
12	Skitter Pop SP-7	0	Surface	Chugger	Good size for lakes	F	P	Bibless	0.54	Nose	$1/4$	$2^3/4$	$3^1/8$
13	Saltwater Chug Bug 8 cm	0	Surface	Chugger	Stronger hooks better	F	P	Bibless	0.65	Nose	$3/8$	$3^1/4$	$3^1/2$
14	Rattlin' Chug Bug	0	Surface	Chugger	Rattles add to commotion		P	Bibless	0.65	Nose	$3/8$	$3^1/4$	$3^1/2$
15	Lucky 13	0	Surface	Chugger	Good standby	F	P	Bibless	0.85	Nose	$5/8$	$3^1/2$	$3^7/8$
16	Skitter Pop SP-9	0	Surface	Chugger	Larger size for bigger fish	F	P	Bibless	0.65	Nose	$1/2$	$3^1/2$	$3^7/8$
17	Teeny Torpedo	0	Surface	Fizzer	Great fizzer in small size	F	P	Bibless	0.74	1 prop	$3/32$	$1^3/8$	$1^3/4$
18	Tiny Torpedo	0	Surface	Fizzer	Great bass lure	F	P	Bibless	0.96	1 prop	$3/16$	$1^7/8$	$2^3/8$
19	Turbo #1	0	Surface	Fizzer	Value for money	F	P	Bibless	0.89	1 prop	$1/4$	$1^7/8$	$2^3/8$
20	Sputterbuzz	0	Surface	Fizzer	Maximum surface action		P	Bibless	1.24	1 prop	$3/8$	$2^1/4$	$4^1/8$

1

2

3

5

6

8

9

TROLLING		LURE SOURCE		SIZE	
DEPTH ON 22 ft AT 1.5 KNOTS	DEPTH ON 22 FT AT 2 KNOTS (Test Speed)	MANUFACTURER	COUNTRY OF MANUFACTURE	DESCRIBED SIZE (in)	DESCRIBED WEIGHT (oz)
		The Producers	China	$1^3/_4$	
		Storm	Estonia	$1^5/_8$	$^1/_{16}$
		Rebel	USA	$1^3/_4$	$^1/_8$
		Fred Arbogast	El Salvador		
		Rebel	USA	$2^1/_2$	
		The Producers	China	$2^1/_4$	$^5/_8$
		Rapala	Ireland	2	$^1/_4$
		Storm	Estonia	$2^3/_8$	$^1/_4$
		Rebel	USA	$2^1/_2$	$^1/_4$
		River 2 Sea		$2^1/_2$	
		Berkley	USA	$2^3/_4$	$^5/_{16}$
		Rapala	Ireland	$2^3/_4$	$^1/_4$
		Storm	Estonia	$3^1/_8$	$^3/_8$
		Storm	Estonia	$3^1/_8$	$^3/_8$
		Heddon	El Salvador		
		Rapala	Ireland	$3^1/_2$	$^1/_2$
		Heddon	Mexico		
		Heddon	El Salvador		
		The Producers	China	2	$^3/_8$
		Fred Arbogast	El Salvador		$^1/_4$

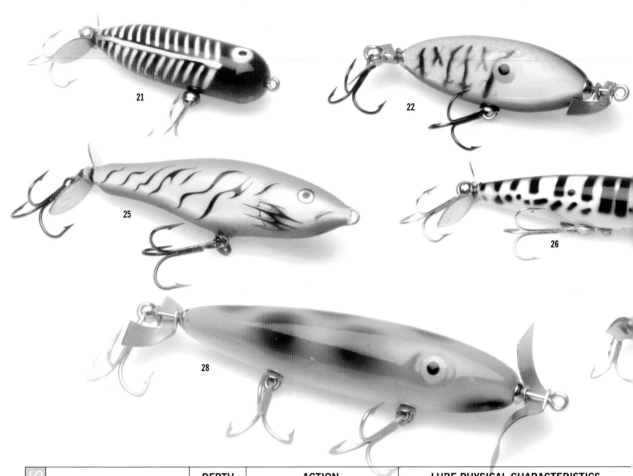

		DEPTH		ACTION		LURE PHYSICAL CHARACTERISTICS							
NUMBER	LURE	DEPTH (FT) ON 66 FT	MAKER'S STATED DEPTH	ACTION	COMMENTS	FLOATING – SINKING – SUSPENDING	BODY MATERIAL PLASTIC – METAL – WOOD – RUBBER	BIB MATERIAL	WIDTH OF BIB (in)	TOW POINT	ACTUAL WEIGHT (oz)	ACTUAL BODY LENGTH (in)	LENGTH WITH BIB (in)
21	Baby Torpedo	0	Surface	Fizzer	Lots of fizz works very well	F	P	Bibless	1.31	1 prop	$^5/_{16}$	$2^3/_8$	$2^7/_8$
22	Woodchopper 3/8 oz	0	Surface	Fizzer	Nose prop lots of noise	F	W	Bibless	1.35	2 prop	$^3/_8$	$2^3/_8$	$3^3/_8$
23	Turbo #2	0	Surface	Fizzer	Alternative to Torpedos	F	P	Bibless	1.23	1 prop	$^5/_{16}$	$2^1/_2$	$2^7/_8$
24	Woodchopper 1/2 oz	0	Surface	Fizzer	Big size for quality fish	F	W	Bibless	1.69	2 prop	$^3/_4$	$3^1/_8$	$4^1/_4$
25	Skitter Prop SPR-7	0	Surface	Fizzer	Nice Rapala fizzer	F	P	Bibless	1.33	1 prop	$^5/_{16}$	$3^1/_8$	$3^1/_2$
26	Dying Flutter	0	Surface	Fizzer	Twin prop successful lure	F	P	Bibless	1.26	2 prop	$^3/_8$	$3^3/_4$	$4^1/_4$
27	Double Ender	0	Surface	Fizzer	Chinese version works ok	F	P	Bibless	1.36	2 prop	$^1/_2$	$3^3/_4$	$4^1/_4$
28	Woodchopper	0	Surface	Fizzer	Pike and musky size	F	W	Bibless	2.16	2 prop	$^7/_8$	4	$5^1/_4$
29	Devil's Horse AF100	0	Surface	Fizzer	Great bass lure	F	P	Bibless	1.05	2 prop	$^3/_8$	$4^1/_8$	$4^3/_4$
30	Jitterbug 1/8 oz	0	Surface	Paddler	Small version takes good fish	F	P	Metal	1.35	Nose	$^1/_8$	$1^1/_2$	$1^3/_4$
31	Jitterbug Clicker 1/4 oz	0	Surface	Paddler	Rattles add to appeal	F	P	Metal	1.44	Nose	$^1/_4$	$1^3/_4$	$2^1/_8$
32	Jitterbug 1/4 oz	0	Surface	Paddler	An absolute must	F	P	Metal	1.43	Nose	$^1/_4$	$1^3/_4$	$2^1/_8$
33	Jitter Mouse 1/8 oz	0	Surface	Paddler	Imitation mouse	F	P	Metal	1.36	Nose	$^1/_8$	$1^3/_4$	2
34	Tiny Crazy Crawler	0	Surface	Paddler	Versatile fantastic lure	F	P	Bibless, metal wings	2.37	Nose	$^1/_4$	$1^3/_4$	$2^1/_8$

THE TEST RESULTS

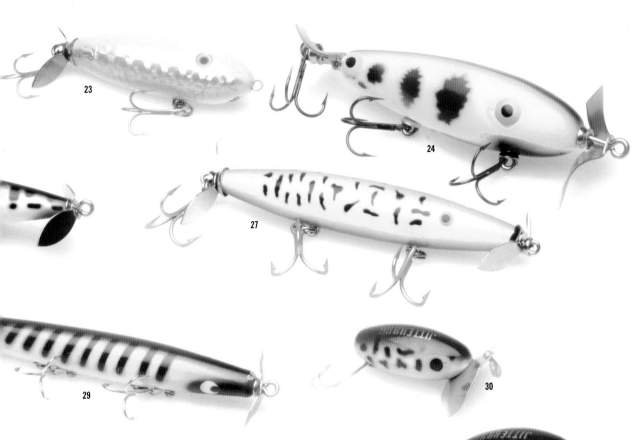

TROLLING		LURE SOURCE		SIZE	
DEPTH ON 22 ft AT 1.5 KNOTS	DEPTH ON 22 FT AT 2 KNOTS (Test Speed)	MANUFACTURER	COUNTRY OF MANUFACTURE	DESCRIBED SIZE (in)	DESCRIBED WEIGHT (oz)
		Heddon	Mexico		
		Luhr Jensen	Mexico		$^3/_8$
		The Producers	China	$2^1/_2$	$^1/_4$
		Luhr Jensen	Mexico		$^1/_2$
		Rapala	Ireland	$2^3/_4$	$^1/_4$
		Heddon	Mexico		
		The Producers	China	$3^3/_4$	$^3/_8$
		Luhr Jensen	Mexico		$^3/_4$
		Smithwick	Mexico	$4^1/_2$	$^3/_8$
		Fred Arbogast	Guatemala		$^1/_8$
		Fred Arbogast	El Salvador		$^1/_4$
		Fred Arbogast	El Salvador		$^1/_4$
		Fred Arbogast	El Salvador		$^1/_8$
		Heddon	Mexico		

		DEPTH		ACTION		LURE PHYSICAL CHARACTERISTICS							
NUMBER	LURE	DEPTH (FT) ON 66 FT	MAKER'S STATED DEPTH	ACTION	COMMENTS	FLOATING – SINKING – SUSPENDING	BODY MATERIAL PLASTIC – METAL– WOOD – RUBBER	BIB MATERIAL	WIDTH OF BIB (in)	TOW POINT	ACTUAL WEIGHT (oz)	ACTUAL BODY LENGTH (in)	LENGTH WITH BIB (in)
35	Cicada Pop 55	0	Surface	Paddler	Incredibly life-like - top lure	F	P	Plastic	1.63	Nose		2$\frac{1}{8}$	2$\frac{3}{16}$
36	Jitterbug Clicker	0	Surface	Paddler	Rattles for extra attraction	F	P	Metal	1.53	Nose	$\frac{3}{8}$	2$\frac{1}{4}$	2$\frac{1}{2}$
37	Bass-A-Rooney	0	Surface	Paddler		F	P	Metal	1.91	Nose	$\frac{5}{16}$	2$\frac{1}{4}$	2$\frac{5}{8}$
38	Jitterbug JTD 3/8 oz	0	Surface	Paddler	Joint adds little extra act	F	P	Metal	1.52	Nose	$\frac{5}{16}$	2$\frac{3}{8}$	2$\frac{3}{4}$
39	Crazy Crawler	0	Surface	Paddler	Special lure that still rates	F	P	Bibless, metal wings	3.63	Nose	$\frac{1}{2}$	2$\frac{1}{2}$	2$\frac{5}{8}$
40	Night Walker	0	Surface	Paddler	Australian version special action	F	P	Plastic	2.07	Nose	$\frac{3}{8}$	2$\frac{1}{2}$	2$\frac{5}{8}$
41	Jitterbug 5/8 oz	0	Surface	Paddler	Bigger size for different s	F	P	Metal	1.69	Nose	$\frac{1}{2}$	2$\frac{5}{8}$	2$\frac{7}{8}$
42	Cicada Pop 70	0	Surface	Paddler	Incredibly life-like, must have lure	F	P	Plastic	2.11	Nose		2$\frac{3}{4}$	2$\frac{7}{8}$
43	Jitterbug JTD 5/8 oz	0	Surface	Paddler	Not a fan of jointed version	F	P	Metal	1.69	Nose	$\frac{5}{8}$	3	3$\frac{1}{2}$
44	XL Jitterbug	0	Surface	Paddler	Saltwater applications as well	F	P	Metal	2.55	Nose	1$\frac{1}{8}$	4$\frac{1}{2}$	4$\frac{7}{8}$
45	Monster Popper F	0	Surface	Popper	Cheap but highly successful		P	Bibless	0.91	Nose	$\frac{7}{8}$	4$\frac{1}{4}$	4$\frac{1}{2}$

35

36

38

39

40

TROLLING		LURE SOURCE		SIZE	
DEPTH ON 22 ft AT 1.5 KNOTS	DEPTH ON 22 FT AT 2 KNOTS (Test Speed)	MANUFACTURER	COUNTRY OF MANUFACTURE	DESCRIBED SIZE (in)	DESCRIBED WEIGHT (oz)
		River 2 Sea	Japan	$2^1/_8$	$^1/_4$
		Fred Arbogast	El Salvador		$^3/_8$
		The Producers	China	2	$^1/_4$
		Fred Arbogast	El Salvador		$^3/_8$
		Heddon	Mexico		
		Halco	Aust—WA		
		Fred Arbogast	El Salvador		$^5/_8$
		River 2 Sea	Japan	$2^3/_4$	$^1/_2$
		Fred Arbogast	El Salvador		$^5/_8$
		Fred Arbogast	El Salvador		$1^1/_4$
		The Producers	China	$4^1/_4$	1

41

42

43

37

44

45

NUMBER	LURE	DEPTH (FT) ON 66 FT	MAKER'S STATED DEPTH	ACTION	COMMENTS	FLOATING – SINKING – SUSPENDING	BODY MATERIAL PLASTIC – METAL – WOOD – RUBBER	BIB MATERIAL	WIDTH OF BIB (in)	TOW POINT	ACTUAL WEIGHT (oz)	ACTUAL BODY LENGTH (in)	LENGTH WITH BIB (in)
46	Saltwater Chug Bug	0	Surface	Popper	First rate saltwater popper		P	Bibless	0.93	Nose	$7/8$	$4^3/8$	$4^5/8$
47	Skitter Pop SSP-12	0	Surface	Popper	Watch hardware for big fish	F	P	Bibless	0.89	Nose	$1^3/8$	5	$5^3/8$
48	Pencil Popper Small	0	Surface	Popper	Long casting capacity	S	P	Bibless	0.55	Nose	$1^1/8$	$5^3/4$	6
49	Pencil Popper Large	0	Surface	Popper	Great popper – sinks at rest	S	P	Bibless	0.69	Nose	$1^5/8$	$6^1/2$	$6^3/4$
50	Mini-Me Ghost F	0	Surface	Stick bait		F	P	Bibless		Nose	$3/8$	$2^1/2$	$2^5/8$
51	Spit'n Image Jr	0	Surface	Stick bait	Popular and successful bait	F	P	Bibless		Nose	$3/8$	$2^7/8$	$3^1/8$
52	Spit'n Image	0	Surface	Stick bait	Very good lure	F	P	Bibless		Nose	$1/2$	$3^1/4$	$3^1/2$
53	Floating Mullet BM7	0	Surface	Stick bait	Tow point on top of nose	F	P	Bibless		Body	$3/8$	$3^5/8$	$3^5/8$
54	Bubble 100	0	Surface	Stick bait	Nice finish to lure	F	P	Bibless		Nose	$1/2$	$3^7/8$	$4^1/8$
55	Ghost F	0	Surface	Stick bait	Others recommended higher	F	P	Bibless		Nose	$5/8$	$4^1/4$	$4^3/8$
56	Thunder Dog	0	Surface	Stick bait	Great lure	F	P	Bibless		Nose	$5/8$	$4^3/8$	$4^1/2$

46

48

50

51

TROLLING		LURE SOURCE		SIZE	
DEPTH ON 22 ft AT 1.5 KNOTS	DEPTH ON 22 FT AT 2 KNOTS (Test Speed)	MANUFACTURER	COUNTRY OF MANUFACTURE	DESCRIBED SIZE (in)	DESCRIBED WEIGHT (oz)
		Storm	Estonia	$4^3/_8$	$^7/_8$
		Rapala	Ireland	$4^3/_4$	$1^3/_8$
		Cotton Cordell	USA		
		Cotton Cordell	El Salvador		
		The Producers	China	$2^1/_2$	$^5/_{16}$
		Excalibur	El Salvador		
		Excalibur	El Salvador		
		Bomber	El Salvador	$3^1/_2$	$^5/_8$
		River 2 Sea		4	
		The Producers	China	$4^1/_4$	$^3/_4$
		Storm	Estonia	$4^3/_8$	$^5/_8$

NUMBER	LURE	DEPTH (FT) ON 66 FT	MAKER'S STATED DEPTH	ACTION	COMMENTS	FLOATING – SINKING – SUSPENDING	BODY MATERIAL PLASTIC – METAL – WOOD – RUBBER	BIB MATERIAL	WIDTH OF BIB (in)	TOW POINT	ACTUAL WEIGHT (oz)	ACTUAL BODY LENGTH (in)	LENGTH WITH BIB (in)
57	Jumpin' Minnow	0	Surface	Stick bait	Old favorite	F	P	Bibless		Nose	$^3/_4$	$4^1/_2$	$4^7/_8$
58	Mega Ghost	0	Surface	Stick bait	Watch split rings with big fish	F	P	Bibless		Nose	1	$5^1/_8$	$5^1/_8$
59	Aglia Size 1	3"		Spinner	Fantastic light spinner	S	M	Spinner		Nose	$^3/_{16}$	$1^1/_4$	
60	Twisty 5 g	6"		Tight roll	Great all around light lure	S	M	Bibless	0.16	Body	$^3/_{16}$	$1^7/_8$	$1^7/_8$
61	Wobbler 20 g Sparkler	9"		Medium wobble	Good casting lure espially in salt	S	M	Bibless	0.09	Nose	$^7/_8$	$2^5/_8$	$2^5/_8$
62	Aglia TW 1 Streamer	9"		Spinner	Spinner on fly body	S	M	Bibless			$^1/_8$		
63	Bang-O-Lure #5	9"		Tight sway, medium roll	Great combination in very shallow lure	F	W	Plastic	0.50	Nose	$^3/_8$	$5^1/_8$	$5^1/_2$
64	Little Tasmanian Devil 7 g	1'		Medium wobble	Very good lure troll or cast	S	P	Bibless	0.24	Nose	$^1/_4$	$1^1/_2$	$1^3/_4$
65	Hexagon Sparkler 10 g	1'		Tight wobble	Good saltwater lure	S	M	Bibless	0.26	Nose	$^3/_8$	$1^3/_4$	$1^5/_8$
66	Wobbler 10 g Sparkler	1'		Medium wobble	Great action. Great lure	S	M	Bibless	0.08	Nose	$^5/_{16}$	$1^7/_8$	$1^7/_8$
67	Tasmanian Devil	1'		Medium wobble	Can also be used as vertical jig	S	P	Bibless		Nose	$^1/_4$		

57

59

60

61

TROLLING		LURE SOURCE		SIZE	
DEPTH ON 22 ft AT 1.5 KNOTS	DEPTH ON 22 FT AT 2 KNOTS (Test Speed)	MANUFACTURER	COUNTRY OF MANUFACTURE	DESCRIBED SIZE (in)	DESCRIBED WEIGHT (oz)
		Rebel	Mexico	3$\frac{1}{2}$	$\frac{3}{8}$
		The Producers	China	5$\frac{1}{8}$	1$\frac{1}{8}$
	2"	Mepps Lures	France		
	2"	Halco	Aust–WA		$\frac{3}{16}$
	4"	Halco	Aust–WA		$\frac{3}{4}$
	4"	Mepps Lures	France		$\frac{1}{8}$
	4"	Bagley	Dominican Rep		
	6"	Wigston's	Aust–Tas		$\frac{1}{4}$
	6"	Halco	Aust–WA		$\frac{3}{8}$
	6"	Halco	Aust–WA		$\frac{3}{8}$
	6"	Wigston's	Aust–Tas		$\frac{1}{4}$

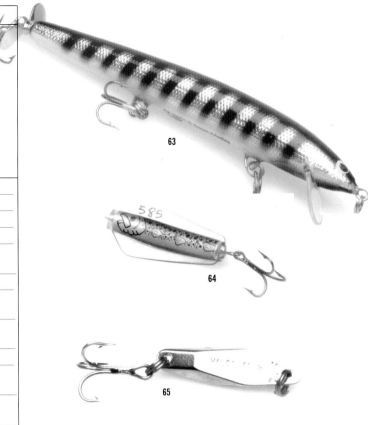

63

64

65

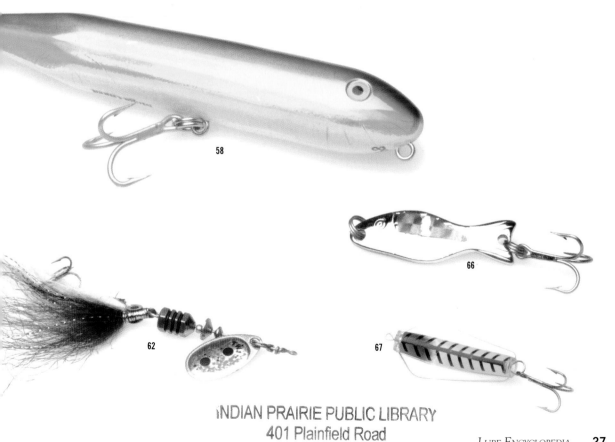

58

62

66

67

		DEPTH		ACTION		LURE PHYSICAL CHARACTERISTICS								
NUMBER	LURE	DEPTH (FT) ON 66 FT	MAKER'S STATED DEPTH	ACTION	COMMENTS	FLOATING – SINKING – SUSPENDING	BODY MATERIAL PLASTIC – METAL– WOOD – RUBBER	BIB MATERIAL	WIDTH OF BIB (in)	TOW POINT	ACTUAL WEIGHT (oz)	ACTUAL BODY LENGTH (in)	LENGTH WITH BIB (in)
68	Streaker 10 g	1'		Tight wobble, tight pitch	Good also with downriggers	S	M	Bibless	0.32	Nose	$^3/_8$	$1^3/_4$	$1^3/_4$
69	Kwikfish K9	1'		Wide sway	Great trout lure	F	P		0.74	Body	$^1/_4$	2	$2^7/_8$
70	Wobbler 30 g Sparkler	1'3"		Medium wobble	Tuna, bluefish etc	S	M	Bibless	0.11	Nose	$1^1/_8$	$2^5/_8$	$2^5/_8$
71	Wobbler 40 g Sparkler	1' 6" wobble		Medium	Good all rounder	S	M	Bibless	0.11	Nose	1	$2^3/_4$	$2^3/_4$
72	Big Ant	1' 6"	2'	Fast sway	Sensitive to speed	F	P	P	0.56	Bib	$^3/_{32}$	$1^1/_4$	$1^5/_8$
73	Bang-O-Lure #4	1' 6"		Medium roll	Good action. Prop turns wel	F	W	Plastic	0.50	Nose	$^5/_{16}$	$4^1/_4$	$4^1/_2$
74	Twisty 15 g	1' 6"		Tight wobble	Good action	S	M	Bibless	0.20	Nose	$^1/_2$	$2^1/_4$	$2^1/_4$
75	Super Vibrax 0	1' 6"		Spinner	Works well at 2 knots.	S	M	Bibless			$^1/_8$		
76	Mini Whacker 1/6 oz	1' 6"		Blade wobble	Needs 1.5 knots or slower.	S	M	Bibless			$^1/_4$		
77	Kwikfish K4	1' 9"		Wide sway	Better at 1.5 knots.	F	P	Bibless		Body	$^3/_{64}$	$1^1/_2$	$1^1/_2$
78	Minnow Spin Super Vibrax 2	2'		Spinner, slow roll	Spinner/Minnow for bigger fish	S	W	Bibless		Nose	$^3/_8$	$3^1/_4$	4

THE TEST RESULTS

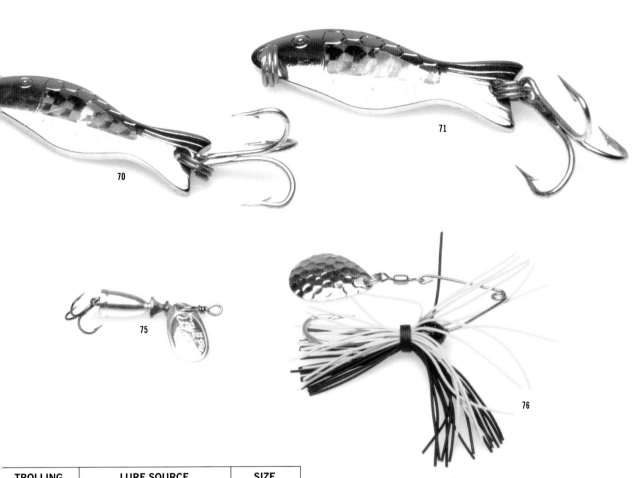

TROLLING		LURE SOURCE		SIZE	
DEPTH ON 22 ft AT 1.5 KNOTS	DEPTH ON 22 FT AT 2 KNOTS (Test Speed)	MANUFACTURER	COUNTRY OF MANUFACTURE	DESCRIBED SIZE (in)	DESCRIBED WEIGHT (oz)
	6"	Halco	Aust–WA		$^3/_8$
	6"	Luhr Jensen	USA	$2^3/_4$	$^1/_4$
	8"	Halco	Aust–WA		$1^3/_8$
	6"	Halco	Aust–WA		1
8"	8"	Rebel	USA	$1^1/_4$	$^3/_{32}$
	8"	Bagley	Dominican Rep		$^1/_4$
	10"	Halco	Aust–WA		$^1/_2$
	10"	Blue Fox	Finland		
	10"	Bomber	El Salvador		$^1/_6$
	10"	Luhr Jensen	USA	$1^1/_2$	$^3/_{64}$
	1'	Blue Fox	Finland		$^3/_8$

NUMBER	LURE	DEPTH (FT) ON 66 FT	MAKER'S STATED DEPTH	ACTION	COMMENTS	FLOATING – SINKING – SUSPENDING	BODY MATERIAL PLASTIC – METAL – WOOD – RUBBER	BIB MATERIAL	WIDTH OF BIB (in)	TOW POINT	ACTUAL WEIGHT (oz)	ACTUAL BODY LENGTH (in)	LENGTH WITH BIB (in)
79	Oxboro Ox Spoon	2'		Wide wobble	Collector lure that works	S	M	Bibless		Nose	$^7/_8$	$3^1/_2$	$3^1/_2$
80	Finlandia S	2'		Shimmy	Swivel affects action.	F	W	Plastic	0.33	Nose	$^1/_{16}$	1	$1^1/_4$
81	Rooster Tail 1/8 oz	2'		Spinner	Good action good lure	S	M	Bibless			$^1/_8$		
82	Super Vibrax 1	2'		Spinner	Top notch spinner	S	M	Bibless			$^1/_8$		
83	Streaker 20 g	2' 3"		Tight wobble, tight pitch	Good fast speed lure	S	M	Bibless	0.31	Nose	$^3/_4$	$2^3/_8$	$2^3/_8$
84	Crawdaddy #0	2' 3"		Wide pitch	Nice small lure	F	P	Plastic	0.42	Nose	$^3/_{32}$	$1^1/_2$	$1^7/_8$
85	Super Vibrax Minnow Spin 2	2' 6"		Spinner		S	M	Bibless		Nose		2	$2^7/_8$
86	Tasmanian Devil 13.5 g	2' 6"		Medium wobble	Larger size, great with dow	S	P	Bibless	0.25	Nose	$^1/_2$	2	$2^3/_8$
87	Streaker 30 g	2' 6"		Medium wobble, tight pitch		S	M	Bibless	0.41	Nose	$1^1/_8$	$2^5/_8$	$2^5/_8$
88	Streaker 40 g	2' 6"		Medium wobble		S	M	Bibless	0.39	Nose	$1^1/_2$	$3^1/_8$	3
89	Nature Hopper 1/8 oz	2' 6"		Spinner	Heavier spinner	S	M	Bibless		Nose	$^1/_8$	$^5/_8$	$1^1/_2$

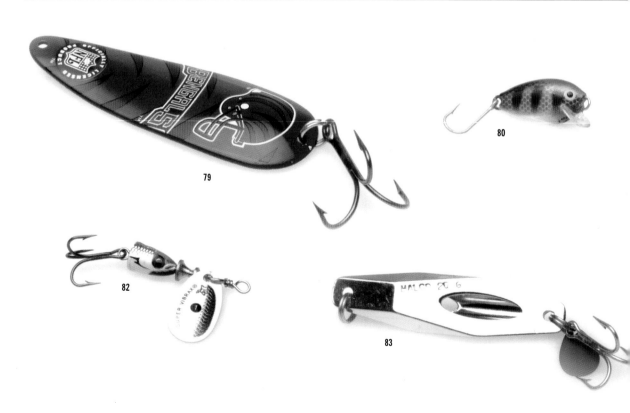

79

80

82

83

TROLLING		LURE SOURCE		SIZE	
DEPTH ON 22 ft AT 1.5 KNOTS	DEPTH ON 22 FT AT 2 KNOTS (Test Speed)	MANUFACTURER	COUNTRY OF MANUFACTURE	DESCRIBED SIZE (in)	DESCRIBED WEIGHT (oz)
	1'	Oxboro Outdoors	USA		
	10"	Nilsmaster	Finland	$1\frac{1}{8}$	$\frac{1}{16}$
	1'	Worden's	USA		$\frac{1}{8}$
	1'	Blue Fox	Finland		
	1'	Halco	Aust–WA		$\frac{3}{4}$
	1'	The Producers	China	$1\frac{5}{8}$	$\frac{1}{8}$
	1' 1"	Blue Fox	Finland		
	1' 1"	Wigston's	Aust–Tas		$\frac{1}{2}$
	1' 1"	Halco	Aust–WA		1
	1' 1"	Halco	Aust–WA		$1\frac{3}{8}$
	1' 1"	Blue Fox	China		$\frac{1}{8}$

85

86

87

81

84

88

89

		DEPTH		ACTION		LURE PHYSICAL CHARACTERISTICS							
NUMBER	LURE	DEPTH (FT) ON 66 FT	MAKER'S STATED DEPTH	ACTION	COMMENTS	FLOATING – SINKING – SUSPENDING	BODY MATERIAL PLASTIC – METAL – WOOD – RUBBER	BIB MATERIAL	WIDTH OF BIB (in)	TOW POINT	ACTUAL WEIGHT (oz)	ACTUAL BODY LENGTH (in)	LENGTH WITH BIB (in)
90	Bang Tail 2 1/8 oz	2' 6"		Spinner		S	M	Bibless			$3/16$		
91	Big Tasmanian Devil	2' 6"		Medium		S	P	Bibless	0.30	Nose	$7/8$	3	$3 3/8$
92	Kwikfish K5	2' 6"		Wide sway		F	P	Bibless	0.46	Body	$1/16$	$1 1/4$	$1 3/4$
93	Tru Track Classic	2' 6"		Blade wobble	Great spinnerbait	S	M	Bibless		Nose	$5/8$		
94	Inkoo 26 g	2' 9"		Medium wobble	Great action. Heavier spoon	S	M	Bibless		Nose	$7/8$	3	3
95	Twisty 20 g	2' 9"		Tight wobble		S	M	Bibless	0.33	Nose	$3/4$	$2 1/2$	$2 1/2$
96	Hexagon Sparkler 20 g	2' 9"		Tight wobble	Good action.	S	M	Bibless	0.32	Nose	$5/8$	$2 1/4$	$2 1/4$
97	Super Vibrax 2	2' 9"		Spinner	Great spinner	S	M	Bibless			$3/16$		
98	Rooster Tail 1/6 oz	2' 9"		Spinner	Great spinner	S	M	Bibless			$1/4$		
99	Super Vibrax 4	2' 9"		Spinner		S	M	Bibless			$3/8$		
100	Bushwacker 1/4 oz	2' 9"		Blade wobble		S	M	Bibless			$1/2$		

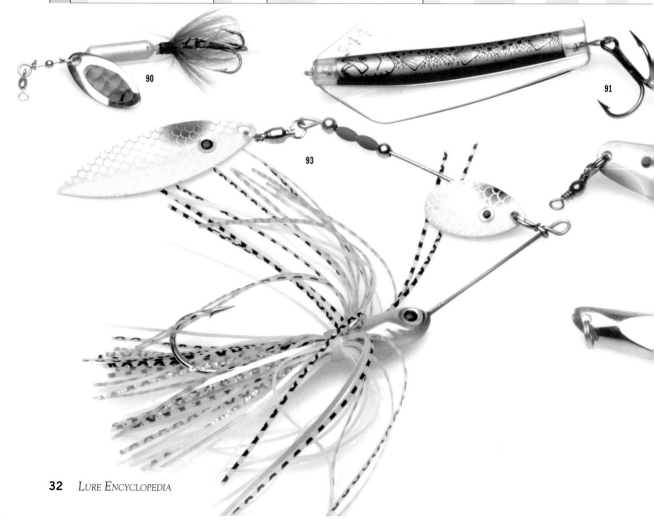

TROLLING		LURE SOURCE		SIZE	
DEPTH ON 22 ft AT 1.5 KNOTS	DEPTH ON 22 FT AT 2 KNOTS (Test Speed)	MANUFACTURER	COUNTRY OF MANUFACTURE	DESCRIBED SIZE (in)	DESCRIBED WEIGHT (oz)
	1' 1"	Luhr Jensen	Mexico		$1/8$
1' 1"	1'	Wigston's	Aus–Tas	$7/8$	
	1' 1"	Luhr Jensen	USA	$1 3/4$	$1/16$
1' 4"		Andreas Tackle	USA		$3/8$
1' 4"		Blue Fox	Finland	3	$7/8$
	1' 1"	Halco	Aust–WA		$3/4$
	1' 1"	Halco	Aust–WA		$3/4$
	1' 4"	Blue Fox	Finland		
	1' 4"	Worden's	Mexico		$3/16$
	1' 4"	Blue Fox	Finland		
	1' 4"	Bomber	El Salvador		$1/4$

96

97

98

99

92

94

95

100

NUMBER	LURE	DEPTH (FT) ON 66 FT	MAKER'S STATED DEPTH	ACTION	COMMENTS	FLOATING – SINKING – SUSPENDING	BODY MATERIAL PLASTIC – METAL – WOOD – RUBBER	BIB MATERIAL	WIDTH OF BIB (in)	TOW POINT	ACTUAL WEIGHT (oz)	ACTUAL BODY LENGTH (in)	LENGTH WITH BIB (in)
		DEPTH		**ACTION**		**LURE PHYSICAL CHARACTERISTICS**							
101	Hexagon Sparkler 30 g	3'		Tight wobble		S	M	Bibless	0.39	Nose	$1^1/_8$	$2^1/_2$	$2^1/_2$
102	Sub Wart 5 cm	3'	0–1'	Medium sway	Shallow runner in robust profile		P	Plastic	0.59	Nose	$^5/_{16}$	2	$2^1/_8$
103	Super Vibrax 6	3'		Spinner	Large size spinner	S	M	Bibless			$^5/_8$		
104	Minnow Spin Super Vibrax 1	3'		Spinner	Better at 1.5 knots.	S	M	Bibless		Nose	$^1/_8$	$1^3/_{16}$	2
105	Vibrax Minnow Chaser 2	3'		Spinner	Weighted spinner	S	M	Bibless		Nose	$^5/_8$	$2^5/_8$	5
106	Jointed Swim Whizz	3'		Wide sway, wide roll	Great action. Used bottom line attachment	F	P	Plastic	1.12	Bib	$1^7/_8$	$6^1/_2$	$7^3/_4$
107	Teeny Wee Frog	3' 6"	3'	Medium sway	Better at 1.5 knots. Work slowly	F	P	Plastic	0.41	Nose	$^3/_{32}$	$1^1/_2$	$1^5/_8$
108	Mystic Ghost Minnow	3' 6"		Tight roll, tight pitch	Very tight action with small bib	F	P	Plastic	0.33	Nose	$^3/_{32}$	$2^1/_4$	$2^1/_2$
109	Super Vibrax 3	3' 6"		Spinner		S	M	Bibless			$^1/_4$		
110	Salty Tasmanian Devil	3' 6"		Wide wobble, wide pitch	Great action at 2.5 knots.		P	Bibless	0.16	Nose	$1^1/_2$	$2^1/_8$	$2^1/_8$
111	Pin's Minnow	3' 6"		Shimmy	Great lure but speed sensitive	F	P	Plastic	0.27	Nose	$^1/_{16}$	$2^1/_8$	$2^3/_8$
112	Jointed Minnow J-5	3' 9"		Shimmy, tight pitch	Jointed. Not my favorite Rapala	F	W	Plastic	0.33	Nose	$^1/_8$	$2^1/_4$	$2^1/_2$
113	Sub Wart	3' 9"	0–1'	Wide sway	Excellent lure		P	Plastic	0.47	Nose	$^3/_{16}$	$1^5/_8$	$1^7/_8$
114	Humbug Min 45S	3' 9"		Tight sway	Better at 1.5 knots.	S	P	Plastic	0.39	Nose	$^3/_{16}$	$1^3/_4$	$1^7/_8$

101

102

104

105

106

TROLLING		LURE SOURCE		SIZE	
DEPTH ON 22 ft AT 1.5 KNOTS	DEPTH ON 22 FT AT 2 KNOTS (Test Speed)	MANUFACTURER	COUNTRY OF MANUFACTURE	DESCRIBED SIZE (in)	DESCRIBED WEIGHT (oz)
	1' 4"	Halco	Aust—WA		1
	1' 4"	Storm	Estonia	2	$1/4$
	1' 6"	Blue Fox	Finland		
1' 7"	8"	Blue Fox	Finland		$1/8$
	1' 6"	Blue Fox	Finland		$5/8$
	1' 6"	Homer Le Blanc	USA		
	1' 6"	Rebel	Mexico	$1^1/_2$	$3/_{32}$
	1' 7"	Rebel	Mexico		
	1' 7"	Blue Fox	Finland		
	1' 6"	Wigston's	Aust—Tas		$1^3/_8$
	1' 6"	Yo-Zuri Lures	Japan	2	$1/_{16}$
	1' 10"	Rapala	Ireland	2	$1/8$
	1' 10"	Storm	Estonia	$1^5/_8$	$3/_{16}$
	1' 10"	River 2 Sea		$1^3/_4$	

108

109

110

111

112

113

114

103

107

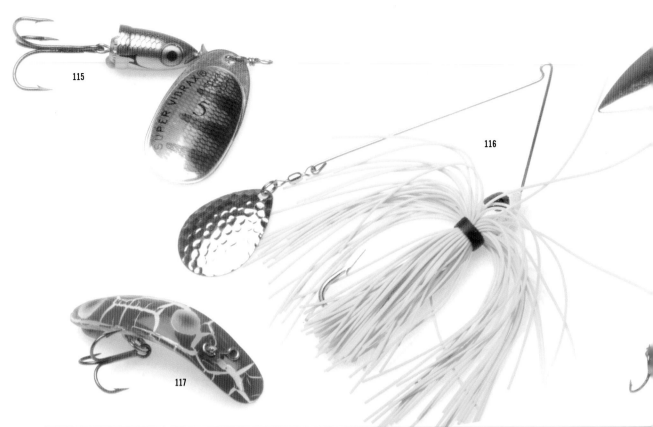

115

116

117

NUMBER	LURE	DEPTH		ACTION		LURE PHYSICAL CHARACTERISTICS							
		DEPTH (FT) ON 66 FT	MAKER'S STATED DEPTH	ACTION	COMMENTS	FLOATING – SINKING – SUSPENDING	BODY MATERIAL PLASTIC – METAL– WOOD – RUBBER	BIB MATERIAL	WIDTH OF BIB (in)	TOW POINT	ACTUAL WEIGHT (oz)	ACTUAL BODY LENGTH (in)	LENGTH WITH BIB (in)
115	Super Vibrax 5	3' 9"		Spinner		S	M	Bibless			$^3/_8$		
116	Bushwacker 3/8 oz	3' 9"		Blade	Lots of blade action. wobble	S	M	Bibless					
117	Kwikfish K7	4'		Wide sway	Better slower–can go even slower than 1.5 knots	F	P	Plastic	0.57	Body	$^1/_8$	$1^5/_8$	$2^3/_8$
118	Tumbleweed Charlie's Spinnerbait 3/8 oz	4'		Blade wobble		S	M	Bibless			$^5/_8$		
119	Jointed Minnow J-7	4' 3"		Shimmy	Good action for jointed lure.	F	W	Plastic	0.42	Nose	$^1/_8$	$2^3/_4$	3
120	Humbug Min 45F	4' 3"		Tight sway	Very good action. Better at 1.5 knots. Some lateral action.	F	P	Plastic	0.41	Nose	$^1/_8$	$1^3/_4$	$1^7/_8$
121	Roscoe's Shiner 5	4' 3"		Medium roll	Can be difficult to tune	F	P	Plastic	0.74	Nose	$^3/_8$	$4^1/_4$	$4^5/_8$
122	Shallow A	4' 3"		Tight sway	Robust profile	F	P	Plastic	0.68	Nose	$^3/_8$	2	$2^1/_4$
123	Vibrax Minnow Chaser	14' 6"		Spinner	Better at 2 knots.	S	W	Bibless		Nose	$^3/_8$	$1^1/_2$	$3^7/_8$
124	Hexagon Sparkler 55 g	4' 6"		Medium wobble	Can also be used as vertical jig.	S	M	Bibless	0.50	Nose	2	3	3
125	Humbug Min 65F	4' 6"		Tight sway, tight roll		F	P	Plastic	0.39	Nose	$^5/_{16}$	$2^5/_8$	$2^7/_8$
126	Bang Tail 4	4' 6"		Spinner	Good action.	S	M	Bibless			$^5/_{16}$		

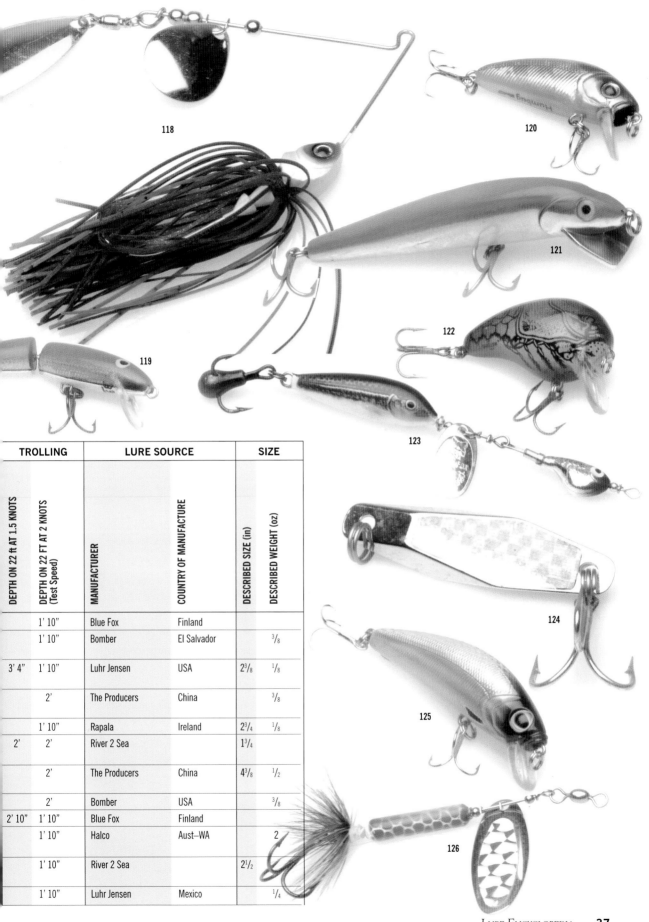

TROLLING		LURE SOURCE		SIZE	
DEPTH ON 22 ft AT 1.5 KNOTS	DEPTH ON 22 FT AT 2 KNOTS (Test Speed)	MANUFACTURER	COUNTRY OF MANUFACTURE	DESCRIBED SIZE (in)	DESCRIBED WEIGHT (oz)
	1' 10"	Blue Fox	Finland		
	1' 10"	Bomber	El Salvador		$^3/_8$
3' 4"	1' 10"	Luhr Jensen	USA	$2^3/_8$	$^1/_8$
	2'	The Producers	China		$^3/_8$
	1' 10"	Rapala	Ireland	$2^3/_4$	$^1/_8$
2'	2'	River 2 Sea		$1^3/_4$	
	2'	The Producers	China	$4^3/_8$	$^1/_2$
	2'	Bomber	USA		$^3/_8$
2' 10"	1' 10"	Blue Fox	Finland		
	1' 10"	Halco	Aust–WA		2
	1' 10"	River 2 Sea		$2^1/_2$	
	1' 10"	Luhr Jensen	Mexico		$^1/_4$

NUMBER	LURE	DEPTH (FT) ON 66 FT	MAKER'S STATED DEPTH	ACTION	COMMENTS	FLOATING – SINKING – SUSPENDING	BODY MATERIAL PLASTIC – METAL– WOOD – RUBBER	BIB MATERIAL	WIDTH OF BIB (in)	TOW POINT	ACTUAL WEIGHT (oz)	ACTUAL BODY LENGTH (in)	LENGTH WITH BIB (in)
127	Kill'r B-II Super Shallow	4' 6"	0–1'	Tight sway	Runs deeper than claimed but good.	F	W	Plastic	0.67	Nose	$3/8$	$2^3/8$	$2^3/4$
128	Tru Track Pro 3/4 oz	4' 6"		Blade wobble		S	M	Bibless		Nose	$1^1/8$		
129	Original Minnow 3	4' 9"		Fast tight sway, tight roll	Classic trout lure	F	P	Plastic	0.40	Nose	$1/16$	$1^1/2$	$1^3/4$
130	Crickhopper 1/8 oz	4' 9"	0–3'	Tight roll	Needs 1.5 knots or slower.	F	P	Plastic	0.57	Bib	$1/8$	$1^3/4$	$2^1/4$
131	Elmo's Zipfish #2	4' 9"		Medium sway	Works well at 2 knots unlike some other simliar lures.	F	P	Bibless	0.52	Body	$3/32$	2	2
132	Stretch 1 Minus	4' 9"		Slow roll	Good big fish lure	F	P	Plastic	0.74	Nose	$5/8$	$4^3/8$	$4^3/4$
133	Snap Shad super small	5'		Shimmy	Good quality dependable small lure		P	Plastic	0.46	Bib	$3/32$	$1^5/8$	$2^1/4$
134	Pro's Choice Minnow	5'		Tight roll	Speed sensitive		P	Plastic	0.35	Nose	$3/16$	$3^1/8$	$3^3/8$
135	MMLS Crankbait	5'		Tight sway	Good action for jointed lure.		P	Metal	0.31	Bib	$1/16$	$1^5/8$	2
136	Countdown Minnow CD3	5'		Shimmy	Great lure	S	W	Plastic	0.42	Nose	$1/8$	$1^1/2$	$1^3/4$
137	Original Minnow 5	5'		Shimmy	Another classic Rapala	F	W	Plastic	0.39	Nose	$5/64$	2	$2^1/4$
138	3-D Fingerling Suspend	5'	6'	Tight roll	Good lure with rippin' qualities	Sus	P	Plastic	0.36	Bib	$1/4$	$2^3/4$	$3^1/4$
139	Humbug Min 65S	5'		Tight sway, tight roll		S	P	Plastic	0.39	Nose	$3/16$	66	72.5
140	TD Hyper Minnow	5'	6' 6"	Medium roll	High quality Japanese lures	Sus	P	Metal	0.48	Bib	$3/16$	$2^3/4$	$3^5/8$

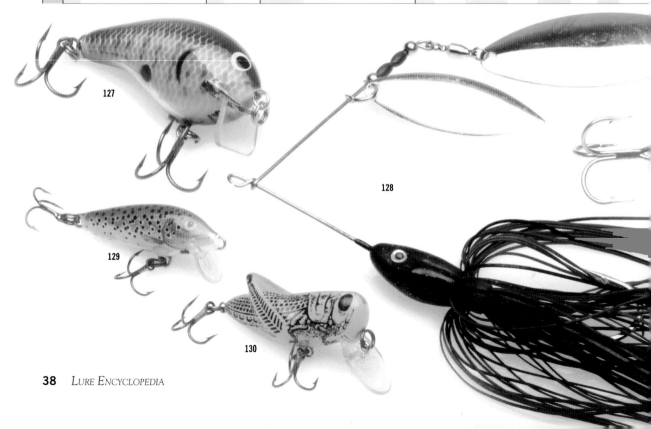

127

128

129

130

TROLLING		LURE SOURCE		SIZE	
DEPTH ON 22 ft AT 1.5 KNOTS	DEPTH ON 22 FT AT 2 KNOTS (Test Speed)	MANUFACTURER	COUNTRY OF MANUFACTURE	DESCRIBED SIZE (in)	DESCRIBED WEIGHT (oz)
	2' 1"	Bagley	Dominican Rep		$3/8$
	2' 4"	Andreas Tackle	USA		$3/4$
	2'	Rapala	Ireland	$1 1/8$	$1/16$
2' 4"	2' 1"	Rebel	USA	$1 1/2$	$3/32$
	2' 4"	The Producers	China	2	$3/32$
	2' 1"	Mann's Lures	USA		
	2'	Yo-Zuri Lures	Japan	$1 5/8$	$3/32$
	2'	Stanley Jigs	China		
	2'	L&S Lures Mirrolures	Costa Rica	$1 5/8$	$1/16$
	2'	Rapala	Ireland	$1 1/8$	$1/8$
	2'	Rapala	Ireland	2	$3/32$
	2'	Yo-Zuri Lures	Japan	$2 3/4$	$1/4$
	2'	River 2 Sea		$2 1/2$	
	2'	Team Diawa	Japan	$2 3/4$	$3/16$

134

135

136

137

138

131

139

133

132

140

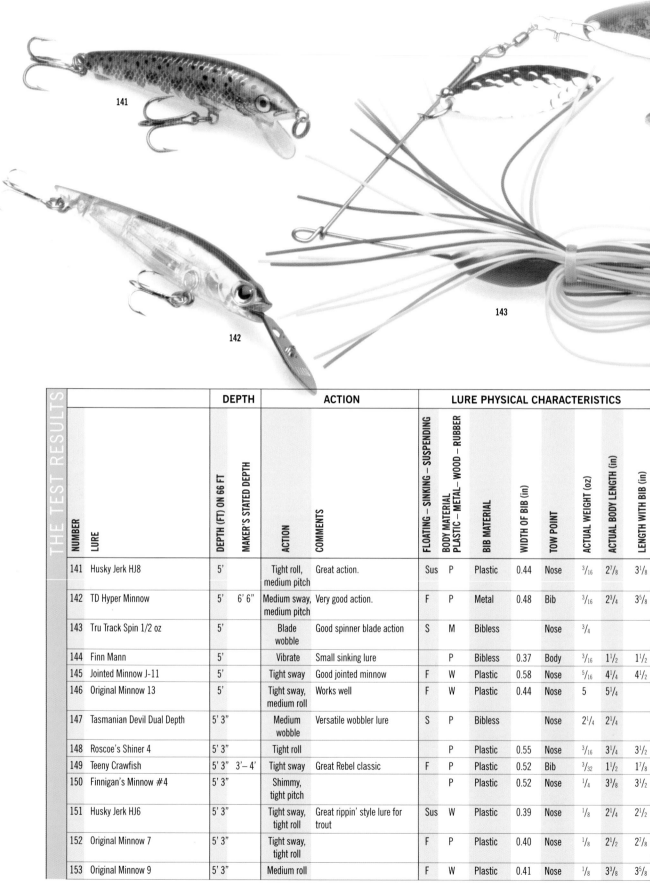

		DEPTH		ACTION		LURE PHYSICAL CHARACTERISTICS							
NUMBER	LURE	DEPTH (FT) ON 66 FT	MAKER'S STATED DEPTH	ACTION	COMMENTS	FLOATING – SINKING – SUSPENDING	BODY MATERIAL PLASTIC – METAL– WOOD – RUBBER	BIB MATERIAL	WIDTH OF BIB (in)	TOW POINT	ACTUAL WEIGHT (oz)	ACTUAL BODY LENGTH (in)	LENGTH WITH BIB (in)
141	Husky Jerk HJ8	5'		Tight roll, medium pitch	Great action.	Sus	P	Plastic	0.44	Nose	$^3/_{16}$	$2^7/_8$	$3^1/_8$
142	TD Hyper Minnow	5'	6' 6"	Medium sway, medium pitch	Very good action.	F	P	Metal	0.48	Bib	$^3/_{16}$	$2^3/_4$	$3^5/_8$
143	Tru Track Spin 1/2 oz	5'		Blade wobble	Good spinner blade action	S	M	Bibless		Nose	$^3/_4$		
144	Finn Mann	5'		Vibrate	Small sinking lure		P	Bibless	0.37	Body	$^3/_{16}$	$1^1/_2$	$1^1/_2$
145	Jointed Minnow J-11	5'		Tight sway	Good jointed minnow	F	W	Plastic	0.58	Nose	$^5/_{16}$	$4^1/_4$	$4^1/_2$
146	Original Minnow 13	5'		Tight sway, medium roll	Works well	F	W	Plastic	0.44	Nose	5	$5^1/_4$	
147	Tasmanian Devil Dual Depth	5' 3"		Medium wobble	Versatile wobbler lure	S	P	Bibless		Nose	$2^1/_4$	$2^1/_4$	
148	Roscoe's Shiner 4	5' 3"		Tight roll			P	Plastic	0.55	Nose	$^3/_{16}$	$3^1/_4$	$3^1/_2$
149	Teeny Crawfish	5' 3"	3'– 4'	Tight sway	Great Rebel classic	F	P	Plastic	0.52	Bib	$^3/_{32}$	$1^1/_2$	$1^7/_8$
150	Finnigan's Minnow #4	5' 3"		Shimmy, tight pitch			P	Plastic	0.52	Nose	$^1/_4$	$3^3/_8$	$3^1/_2$
151	Husky Jerk HJ6	5' 3"		Tight sway, tight roll	Great rippin' style lure for trout	Sus	W	Plastic	0.39	Nose	$^1/_8$	$2^1/_4$	$2^1/_2$
152	Original Minnow 7	5' 3"		Tight sway, tight roll		F	P	Plastic	0.40	Nose	$^1/_8$	$2^1/_2$	$2^7/_8$
153	Original Minnow 9	5' 3"		Medium roll		F	W	Plastic	0.41	Nose	$^1/_8$	$3^3/_8$	$3^5/_8$

THE TEST RESULTS

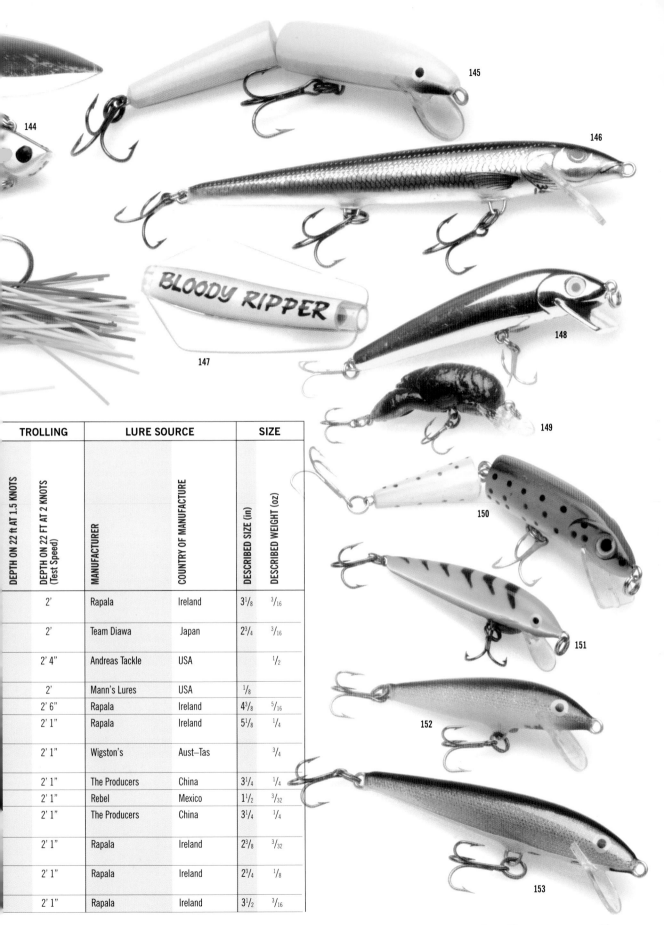

144

145

146

BLOODY RIPPER

147

148

149

150

151

152

153

TROLLING		LURE SOURCE		SIZE	
DEPTH ON 22 ft AT 1.5 KNOTS	DEPTH ON 22 FT AT 2 KNOTS (Test Speed)	MANUFACTURER	COUNTRY OF MANUFACTURE	DESCRIBED SIZE (in)	DESCRIBED WEIGHT (oz)
	2'	Rapala	Ireland	$3^1/_8$	$^3/_{16}$
	2'	Team Diawa	Japan	$2^3/_4$	$^3/_{16}$
	2' 4"	Andreas Tackle	USA		$^1/_2$
	2'	Mann's Lures	USA	$^1/_8$	
	2' 6"	Rapala	Ireland	$4^3/_8$	$^5/_{16}$
	2' 1"	Rapala	Ireland	$5^1/_8$	$^1/_4$
	2' 1"	Wigston's	Aust–Tas		$^3/_4$
	2' 1"	The Producers	China	$3^1/_4$	$^1/_4$
	2' 1"	Rebel	Mexico	$1^1/_2$	$^3/_{32}$
	2' 1"	The Producers	China	$3^1/_4$	$^1/_4$
	2' 1"	Rapala	Ireland	$2^3/_8$	$^3/_{32}$
	2' 1"	Rapala	Ireland	$2^3/_4$	$^1/_8$
	2' 1"	Rapala	Ireland	$3^1/_2$	$^3/_{16}$

NUMBER	LURE	DEPTH (FT) ON 66 FT	MAKER'S STATED DEPTH	ACTION	COMMENTS	FLOATING – SINKING – SUSPENDING	BODY MATERIAL PLASTIC – METAL – WOOD – RUBBER	BIB MATERIAL	WIDTH OF BIB (in)	TOW POINT	ACTUAL WEIGHT (oz)	ACTUAL BODY LENGTH (in)	LENGTH WITH BIB (in)
154	Bushwacker 1/2 oz	5' 3"		Blade wobble		S	M	Bibless			3/4		
155	Aile Killifish	5' 6"	1' –1' 4	Shimmy	Great action. Better at 1.5 knots.	F	P	Plastic	0.46	Nose	3/64	1 1/8	2
156	Finnigan's Minnow #5	5' 6"		Medium roll			P	Plastic	0.77	Nose	1/2	4 3/8	4 5/8
157	Big Mouth	5' 6"	Casting 3' 4" Trolling 6' 6"	Tight sway, tight roll	Prefer other Nilsmasters		P	Bibless	0.68	Nose	3/16	2 5/8	3
158	Twisty 55 g	5' 6"		Medium wobble, tight pitch	Good large casting lure	S	M	Bibless	0.40	Nose	2	3 1/2	3 1/2
159	RMG Sneaky Bream Scorpion	5' 6"	4' 6"		Absolutely dynamite lure	Sus	P	Plastic	0.48	Bib	3/32	1 5/8	2 1/4
160	Invincible 8	5' 9"	6' 6"	Medium roll	Invincibles fantastic for Australian barramundi	F	W	Plastic	0.50	Nose	3/16	2 7/8	3 1/8
161	RMG Scorpion 35 STD	5' 9"	3' 4"	Tight sway	Much better slower but highly recommended		P	Plastic	0.49	Bib	3/32	1 5/8	2 1/4
162	Shallow Thunder 11	5' 9"	3' – 6'	Slow medium roll	Good big lure		P	Plastic	0.70	Nose	3/4	4 5/8	5
163	Jointed Minnow J-9	6'		Medium pitch		F	W	Plastic	0.59	Nose	1/4	3 1/4	3 5/8
164	Elmo's Zipfish #3	6'		Wide sway	Better at 1.5 knots.	F	P	Plastic	0.69	Body	3/16	2	2 7/8
165	Tasmanian Devil Dual Depth	6'		Wide wobble	Great erratic action.	S	P	Bibless		Nose	2 1/4	2 1/4	

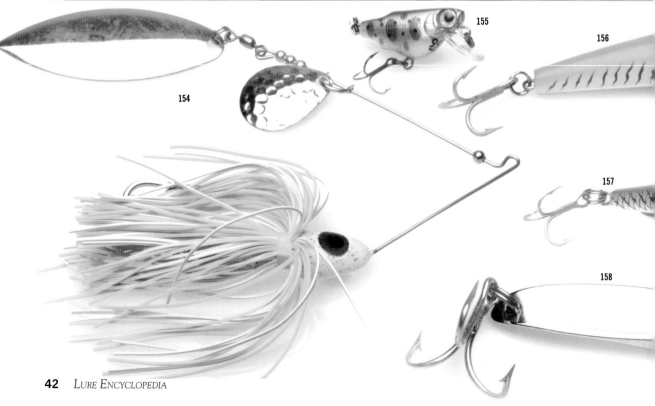

154

155

156

157

158

TROLLING		LURE SOURCE		SIZE	
DEPTH ON 22 ft AT 1.5 KNOTS	DEPTH ON 22 FT AT 2 KNOTS (Test Speed)	MANUFACTURER	COUNTRY OF MANUFACTURE	DESCRIBED SIZE (in)	DESCRIBED WEIGHT (oz)
	2' 1"	Bomber	El Salvador		$\frac{1}{2}$
2' 4"	2' 7"	Yo-Zuri Lures	Japan	$1\frac{1}{8}$	$\frac{1}{16}$
	2' 7"	The Producers	China	$4\frac{1}{4}$	$\frac{3}{8}$
	2' 1"	Nilsmaster	Finland	3	$\frac{3}{16}$
	2' 4"	Halco	Aust—WA		2
	2' 4"	Halco	Aust—WA	$1\frac{3}{8}$	
	2' 4"	Nilsmaster	Finland	$3\frac{1}{8}$	$\frac{1}{4}$
2' 6"	2' 4"	Halco	Aust—WA	$1\frac{3}{8}$	
	2' 4"	Storm	Estonia	$4\frac{3}{8}$	$\frac{3}{4}$
	2' 10"	Rapala	Ireland	$3\frac{1}{2}$	$\frac{1}{4}$
3' 7"	2' 10"	The Producers	China	$2\frac{5}{8}$	$\frac{1}{4}$
	2' 6"	Wigston's	Aust—Tas		$\frac{3}{4}$

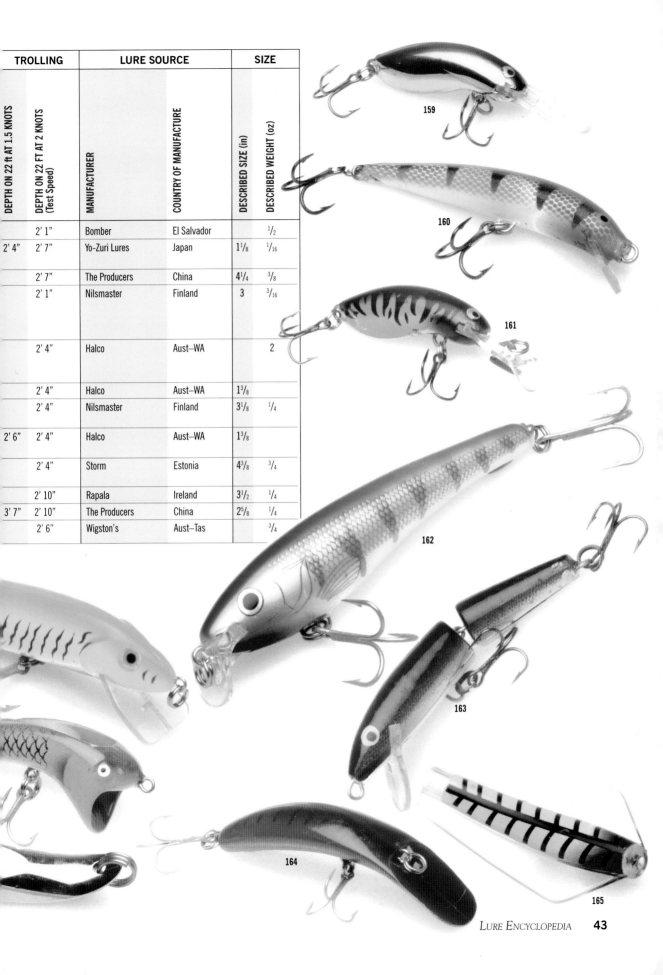

159

160

161

162

163

164

165

		DEPTH		ACTION		LURE PHYSICAL CHARACTERISTICS							
NUMBER	LURE	DEPTH (FT) ON 66 FT	MAKER'S STATED DEPTH	ACTION	COMMENTS	FLOATING – SINKING – SUSPENDING	BODY MATERIAL PLASTIC – METAL – WOOD – RUBBER	BIB MATERIAL	WIDTH OF BIB (in)	TOW POINT	ACTUAL WEIGHT (oz)	ACTUAL BODY LENGTH (in)	LENGTH WITH BIB (in)
166	Salty Tasmanian Devil	6'		Wide wobble, tight pitch	Needs at least 2.5 knots. Cast.	S	P	Bibless	0.51	Nose	$2^3/_4$	3	3
167	Mini Fat Rap	6'		Shimmy	Good lure	S	W	Plastic	0.46	Nose	$^1/_8$	$1^3/_8$	$1^5/_8$
168	Lightning Minnow #1	6'		Slow roll, medium pitch		F	P	Plastic	0.47	Bib	$^1/_8$	2	$2^3/_4$
169	Tru Track Classic 1 oz	6'		Blade wobble	Good blade action	S	M	Bibless		Nose	$1^1/_4$		
170	Kwikfish K8	6' 3"		Wide sway	Needs 1.5 knots or slower.	F	P	Plastic	0.69	Body	$^3/_{16}$	$1^3/_4$	$2^1/_2$
171	Team Esko TE7	6' 6"		Medium roll		F	W	Plastic	0.54	Nose	$^3/_{16}$	$2^5/_8$	3
172	Long Cast Minnow LC12	6' 6"	1' – 4'	Slow roll	Good casting qualities		W	Plastic	0.52	Nose	$^3/_4$	5	$5^3/_8$
173	Countdown Minnow CD5	6' 6"		Fast shimmy	My first choice trout lure	S	W	Plastic	0.43	Nose	$^3/_{16}$	2	$2^1/_4$
174	Rattlin' Rapala RNR-4	6' 6"		Vibrate	Even better with spinner blade attached	S	P	Bibless	0.38	Body	$^3/_{16}$	$1^7/_8$	2
175	Shad Rap Shallow 7	7'		Slow roll	Highly rated	F	W	Plastic	0.57	Nose	$^1/_4$	$2^3/_4$	$3^1/_2$
176	Wee Frog	7'	5' – 7'	Med. sway, tight pitch	Good action but better slow	F	P	Plastic	0.71	Bib	$^1/_4$	$2^1/_4$	$2^1/_2$
177	Honey B Super Shallow	7'	0 – 1'	Shimmy	Not as shallow as advertised	F	W	Plastic	0.51	Nose	$^3/_{16}$	$1^1/_2$	2
178	Crickhopper	7'	0–3'	Tight sway	Speed sensitive	F	P	Plastic	0.56	Bib	$1^1/_2$	$1^7/_8$	

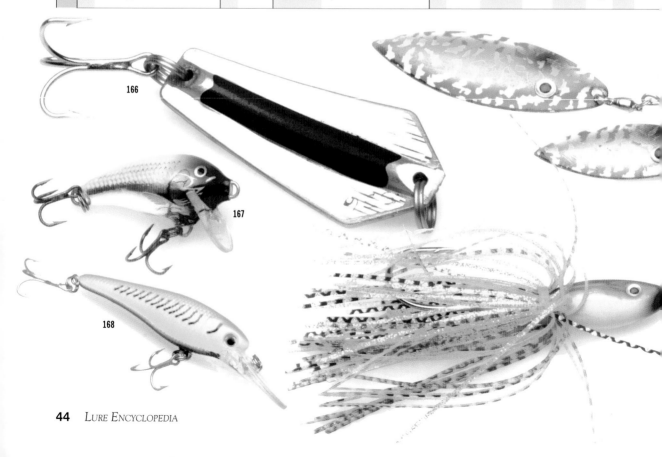

DEPTH ON 22 ft AT 1.5 KNOTS	DEPTH ON 22 FT AT 2 KNOTS (Test Speed)	MANUFACTURER	COUNTRY OF MANUFACTURE	DESCRIBED SIZE (in)	DESCRIBED WEIGHT (oz)
	2' 6"	Wigston's	Aust–Tas	$2^1/_2$	
	2' 6"	Rapala	Ireland	$1^1/_8$	$^1/_8$
	2' 4"	The Producers	China	2	$^3/_{16}$
	2' 6"	Andreas Tackle	USA		1
	3'	Luhr Jensen	USA	$2^1/_2$	$^3/_{16}$
	2' 7"	Rapala	Ireland	$2^3/_4$	$^3/_{16}$
	2' 7"	Rapala	Estonia	$4^3/_4$	$^5/_8$
	2' 10"	Rapala	Ireland	2	$^3/_{16}$
	2' 7"	Rapala	Ireland	$1^5/_8$	$^3/_{16}$
	2' 10"	Rapala	Ireland	$2^3/_4$	$^1/_4$
	2' 10"	Rebel	Mexico	2	$^3/_8$
	2' 10"	Bagley	Dominican Rep		$^1/_4$
	2' 10"	Rebel	USA	$1^1/_2$	$^3/_{32}$

173

174

175

176

177

170

171

178

172

NUMBER	LURE	DEPTH (FT) ON 66 FT	MAKER'S STATED DEPTH	ACTION	COMMENTS	FLOATING – SINKING – SUSPENDING	BODY MATERIAL PLASTIC – METAL – WOOD – RUBBER	BIB MATERIAL	WIDTH OF BIB (in)	TOW POINT	ACTUAL WEIGHT (oz)	ACTUAL BODY LENGTH (in)	LENGTH WITH BIB (in)
179	Laser Pro 190 STD	7'	3' 4"	Med. sway, medium roll	Better at 2.5 knots. Great lure		P	Plastic	0.73	Nose	$1^5/_8$	7	$7^4/_8$
180	Slap-Stick	7'		Med. sway, medium roll	Loud rattle. Very unique design.	F	P	Plastic	0.48	Nose	$^3/_8$	$4^3/_8$	$4^5/_8$
181	Elmo's Zipfish #8	7'		Wide sway	Better at 1.5 knots.	F	P	Plastic	1.40	Body	$1^1/_8$	$3^7/_8$	$5^1/_2$
182	MinMin Shallow	7'	5'	Tight sway	Fantastic for panfish	F	P	Plastic	0.48	Nose	$^1/_8$	2	$2^3/_8$
183	Original Minnow 11	7'		Slow roll	Still a classic	F	W	Plastic	0.44	Nose	$^3/_{16}$	$4^1/_8$	$4^3/_8$
184	Jigger 3	7'		No action—not for trolling	Vertical jigging lure	S	M	Bibless		Body	$^7/_8$	$2^1/_2$	$2^1/_2$
185	Big Bud (Coors)	7'		Medium wide sway	Actually takes fish	F	P	Plastic	0.92	Nose	$^3/_4$	$2^7/_8$	$3^3/_4$
186	Shad Rap Shallow 5	7' 3"		Shimmy	Great trout lure	F	W	Plastic	0.52	Nose	$^1/_4$	$2^1/_4$	$2^3/_4$
187	Laser Pro 45	7' 3"	3' 4"	Fast roll	One of the best lures on the market	F	P	Plastic	0.48	Bib	$^1/_8$	$1^7/_8$	$2^5/_8$
188	Hot Shot 60	7' 3"		Med. sway	Great action at 1.5 knots.	F	P	Plastic	0.44	Body	$^1/_{16}$	$1^1/_4$	$1^7/_8$
189	Thunderstick 6	7' 3"	1'–5'	Tight sway	Good new Storm lure		P	Plastic	0.50	Nose	$^3/_{16}$	$2^1/_2$	$2^7/_8$
190	Humbug Min 90S	7' 3"		Tight roll		S	P	Plastic	0.35	Nose	$^1/_2$	$3^1/_2$	$3^7/_8$
191	Invincible 5	7' 3"	3' 4"	Tight roll	Great versatile lure	F	W	Plastic	0.52	Nose	$^3/_{16}$	$2^1/_8$	$2^1/_4$

179

180

181

182

TROLLING		LURE SOURCE		SIZE	
DEPTH ON 22 ft AT 1.5 KNOTS	DEPTH ON 22 FT AT 2 KNOTS (Test Speed)	MANUFACTURER	COUNTRY OF MANUFACTURE	DESCRIBED SIZE (in)	DESCRIBED WEIGHT (oz)
	2' 4"	Halco	Aust–WA	$7\frac{1}{4}$	$1\frac{5}{8}$
	2' 10"	Bill Lewis Lure	USA		
	3' 4"	The Producers	China	$5\frac{1}{4}$	$1\frac{1}{8}$
	2' 7"	Predatek	Aust–NSW	$\frac{1}{8}$	
	3'	Rapala	Ireland	$4\frac{3}{8}$	$\frac{3}{16}$
	2' 10"	Nilsmaster	Finland	$3\frac{1}{8}$	$\frac{7}{8}$
	3' 1"	Heddon	USA		
	3'	Rapala	Ireland	2	$\frac{3}{16}$
	3'	Halco	Aust–WA	$1\frac{7}{8}$	$\frac{1}{8}$
3' 5"	3'	Luhr Jensen	USA		
	3'	Storm	Estonia	$2\frac{3}{8}$	$\frac{3}{16}$
	3'	River 2 Sea		$3\frac{1}{2}$	
	3'	Nilsmaster	Finland	2	$\frac{3}{16}$

186

187

188

189

184

190

185

191

183

		DEPTH		ACTION		LURE PHYSICAL CHARACTERISTICS							
NUMBER	LURE	DEPTH (FT) ON 66 FT	MAKER'S STATED DEPTH	ACTION	COMMENTS	FLOATING – SINKING – SUSPENDING	BODY MATERIAL PLASTIC – METAL– WOOD – RUBBER	BIB MATERIAL	WIDTH OF BIB (in)	TOW POINT	ACTUAL WEIGHT (oz)	ACTUAL BODY LENGTH (in)	LENGTH WITH BIB (in)
192	Rattlin' Rogue ARB1200	7' 3"	2'	Tight sway, medium roll	Classic American minnow	F	P	Plastic	0.46	Nose	$5/16$	$4^1/2$	$4^3/4$
193	Super Spot	7' 3"		Vibrate	Rattle.	S	P	Bibless	0.28	Body	$3/16$	$2^1/8$	$2^1/8$
194	Rat-L-Trap Tiny Trap	7' 6"		Vibrate	Great for smaller fish	S	P	Bibless	0.51	Body	$3/16$	$1^3/4$	$1^3/4$
195	Master Shad	7' 6"	12'	Very wide sway, medium pitch	Excellent erratic action. Extremely erratic but stable at 1.5 and 2 knots.	S	W	Plastic	1.31	Bib	$1^1/8$	$4^7/8$	$6^1/8$
196	Invincible Jointed 8	7' 6"	6' 6"	Shimmy		F	W	Plastic	0.51	Nose	$1/4$	$3^1/8$	$3^1/2$
197	Big O 1/8 oz	7' 6"		Tight sway		F	P	Plastic	0.43	Nose	$1/8$	$1^5/8$	2
198	Deep Teeny Craw	7' 6"	3'–4'	Tight sway	Much better at 1.5 knots.	F	P	Plastic	0.56	Bib	$3/32$	$1^1/2$	$2^3/8$
199	Bayou Boogie	7' 6"		Vibrate	Oldie but goodie		P	Bibless	0.48	Body	$3/8$	$1^5/8$	$2^1/4$
200	Laser Pro 160 STD	7' 6"	3' 4"	Med. sway, tight roll	Better at 2.5 knots.		P	Bibless	6.48	Nose	1	6	$6^3/8$
201	Tiny N	7' 9"	2'–4'	Tight sway	Versatile lure		P	Plastic	0.51	Nose	$1/8$	$1^5/8$	2
202	Magnum Mag-7	7' 9"		Tight roll	Another top quality Rapala	F	W	Plastic	0.51	Nose	$1/4$	$2^7/8$	$3^1/2$
203	Swim'n Image Shallow Runner	7' 9"		Tight sway, medium roll	Diving version of stick bait		P	Plastic	0.62	Nose	$3/8$	$2^7/8$	$3^1/4$
204	Magnum Mag-9	7' 9"		Medium roll	Great saltwater lure	F	W	Plastic	0.57	Nose	$1/2$	$3^5/8$	$4^1/4$
205	Shad Rap Jointed JSR4	7' 9"	4'–6'	Med.sway	Excellent action—best of Jointed lures tested!		P	Plastic	0.54	Bib	$3/16$	2	3

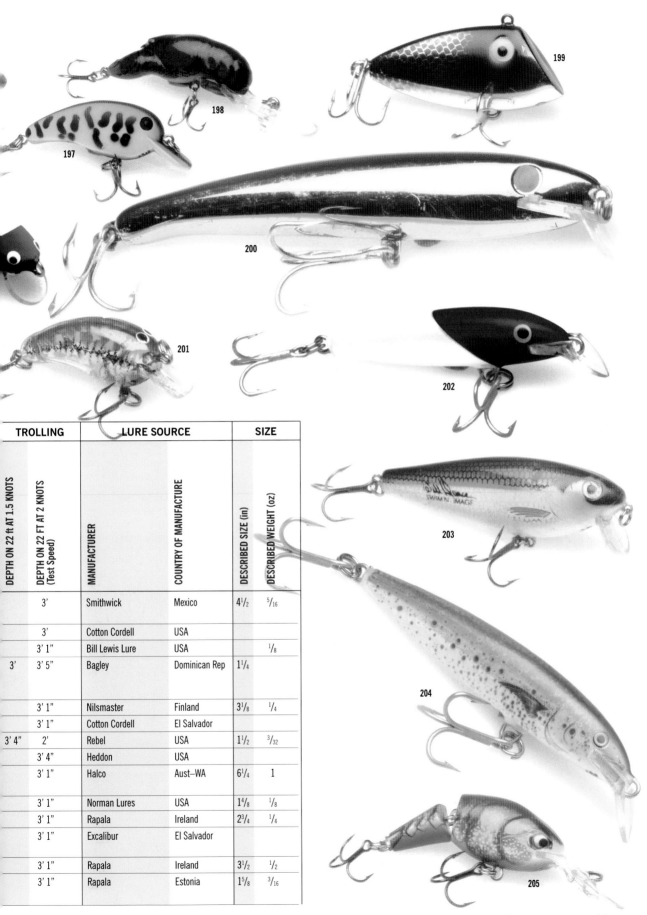

TROLLING		LURE SOURCE		SIZE	
DEPTH ON 22 ft AT 1.5 KNOTS	DEPTH ON 22 FT AT 2 KNOTS (Test Speed)	MANUFACTURER	COUNTRY OF MANUFACTURE	DESCRIBED SIZE (in)	DESCRIBED WEIGHT (oz)
	3'	Smithwick	Mexico	4$^1/_2$	$^5/_{16}$
	3'	Cotton Cordell	USA		
	3' 1"	Bill Lewis Lure	USA		$^1/_8$
3'	3' 5"	Bagley	Dominican Rep	1$^1/_4$	
	3' 1"	Nilsmaster	Finland	3$^1/_8$	$^1/_4$
	3' 1"	Cotton Cordell	El Salvador		
3' 4"	2'	Rebel	USA	1$^1/_2$	$^3/_{32}$
	3' 4"	Heddon	USA		
	3' 1"	Halco	Aust—WA	6$^1/_4$	1
	3' 1"	Norman Lures	USA	1$^4/_8$	$^1/_8$
	3' 1"	Rapala	Ireland	2$^3/_4$	$^1/_4$
	3' 1"	Excalibur	El Salvador		
	3' 1"	Rapala	Ireland	3$^1/_2$	$^1/_2$
	3' 1"	Rapala	Estonia	1$^5/_8$	$^3/_{16}$

		DEPTH		ACTION		LURE PHYSICAL CHARACTERISTICS							
NUMBER	LURE	DEPTH (FT) ON 66 FT	MAKER'S STATED DEPTH	ACTION	COMMENTS	FLOATING – SINKING – SUSPENDING	BODY MATERIAL PLASTIC – METAL– WOOD – RUBBER	BIB MATERIAL	WIDTH OF BIB (in)	TOW POINT	ACTUAL WEIGHT (oz)	ACTUAL BODY LENGTH (in)	LENGTH WITH BIB (in)
206	Triho Min 120F	7' 9"		Tight roll	Big minnow mainly for salt	F	P	Plastic	0.53	Nose	$1/2$	$4^5/8$	5
207	Countdown Minnow CD7	7' 9"		Fast shimmy	Big brown trout lure	S	W	Plastic	0.58	Nose	$1/4$	$2^1/2$	$2^7/8$
208	Long A Minnow 1/2oz	7' 9"		Tight sway, medium roll	Good action.		P	Plastic	0.55	Nose	$3/8$	$4^5/8$	5
209	The Original Pig	8'	3'–6'	Very slow wide sway	Average.	F	W	Bibless		Nose	$3^1/2$	7	$7^3/4$
210	Shallow Sand Viper	8'		Med. sway, tight roll	Try one	F	P	Plastic	0.91	Nose	1	$5^1/2$	$6^1/8$
211	Roscoe's Shiner 7	8'		Med. sway, medium roll	Better at 2.5 knots.		P	Plastic	0.60	Nose	$3/4$	$5^7/8$	$6^1/4$
212	Zero #2	8'		Vibrate		S	P	Bibless		Body	$5/16$	$2^1/2$	$2^1/2$
213	Rattlin' Rapala RNR5	8'		Vibrate	Higher quality	S	P	Bibless	0.40	Body	$3/8$	$2^3/8$	$2^1/2$
214	Klawbaby	8'		Shimmy	Highly regarded crawfish imitation	F	P	Plastic	0.61	Bib	$1/8$	$1^3/8$	$1^3/4$
215	Shad Rap Shallow 8	8'		Med. sway	Great tropical lure	F	W	Plastic	0.57	Nose	$5/16$	$3^1/4$	$3^5/8$
216	Mirashad Fry Size MS50	8'		Tight sway, tight pitch	One of the new generation top notch Japanese lures	Sus	P	Plastic	0.52	Bib	$3/16$	$1^7/8$	$2^5/8$
217	Long A 3/8oz	8'		Med. pitch	Was difficult to tune.		P	Plastic	0.48	Nose	$5/16$	$3^1/4$	$3^3/4$

206

207

208

209

TROLLING		LURE SOURCE		SIZE	
DEPTH ON 22 ft AT 1.5 KNOTS	DEPTH ON 22 FT AT 2 KNOTS (Test Speed)	MANUFACTURER	COUNTRY OF MANUFACTURE	DESCRIBED SIZE (in)	DESCRIBED WEIGHT (oz)
	3' 1"	River 2 Sea		$4^3/_4$	
	3' 1"	Rapala	Ireland	$2^3/_4$	$^1/_4$
	3' 1"	Bomber	Mexico		$^1/_2$
	3' 10"	Odyssey Lures	USA		
	3' 1"	Predatek	Aust–NSW		
	3' 1"	The Producers	China		1
	3' 4"	The Producers	China		
	3' 1"	Rapala	Ireland	2	$^3/_8$
	3' 4"	Luhr Jensen	Mexico		$^1/_8$
	3' 4"	Rapala	Ireland	$3^1/_8$	$^5/_{16}$
	3' 4"	Owner Lures	Japan	2	$^1/_8$
	3' 4"	Bomber	Mexico		$^3/_8$

212

213

214

215

210

216

217

211

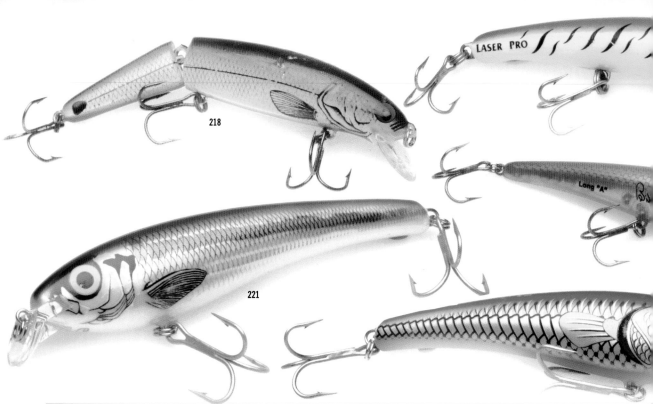

218

221

LASER PRO

Long "A"

		DEPTH		ACTION		LURE PHYSICAL CHARACTERISTICS							
NUMBER	LURE	DEPTH (FT) ON 66 FT	MAKER'S STATED DEPTH	ACTION	COMMENTS	FLOATING – SINKING – SUSPENDING	BODY MATERIAL PLASTIC – METAL– WOOD – RUBBER	BIB MATERIAL	WIDTH OF BIB (in)	TOW POINT	ACTUAL WEIGHT (oz)	ACTUAL BODY LENGTH (in)	LENGTH WITH BIB (in)
218	Jointed Long A	8'		Med. sway	Good action for jointed lure, rattle.		P	Plastic	0.54	Nose	$5/8$	$4^5/8$	5
219	Laser Pro 120 STD	8'	3' 4"	Wide roll	Better faster.		P	Plastic	0.60	Nose	$5/8$	$4^5/8$	$4^7/8$
220	Stanley Minnow	8'		Med. sway, tight roll	Bigger minnow		P	Plastic	0.57	Nose	$1/2$	$4^1/2$	5
221	Shallow Thunder 15	8'	3' 4"–6'	Med.sway, medium roll	Great action.		P	Plastic	0.84	Bib		$5^7/8$	$6^5/8$
222	Long A Select Series	8'		Med. sway, tight roll			P	Plastic	0.57	Nose	$1/2$	$4^5/8$	5
223	Shallow Thunder 15	8'	3' 4"–6'	Tight sway, slow medium roll	Better at 2.5 knots and much faster		P	Plastic	0.84	Nose	$1^1/2$	6	$6^5/8$
224	Balsa B-I	8'	3' 4"–4'	Tight sway, tight pitch	Better at 1.5 knots.	F	W	Plastic	0.92	Nose	$1/2$	$2^1/8$	$2^5/8$
225	Mini Z Shallow	8' 3"		Tight roll, tight pitch	Excellent action.	F	P	Plastic	0.63	Nose	$3/8$	$2^3/8$	$2^1/2$
226	Balsa B-III	8' 3"	0–4'	Med.sway, tight roll	Great stout profile	F	W	Plastic	0.93	Nose	$3/4$	$3^1/8$	$3^1/2$
227	Rat-L-Trap Mini Trap	8' 3"		Vibrate		S	P	Bibless	0.39	Body	$3/8$	$2^1/2$	$2^1/2$
228	Burmek B1 Pike Jointed	8' 3"		Med. sway	Great action. Extra kick on tail section. Musky lure	F	P	Plastic	1.24	Bib	$2^1/4$	$7^3/8$	$8^3/8$
229	Invincible DR5	8' 6"	6' 6"	Tight roll	Under-rated Nilsmaster		W	Plastic	0.67	Nose	$3/16$	$2^1/8$	

THE TEST RESULTS

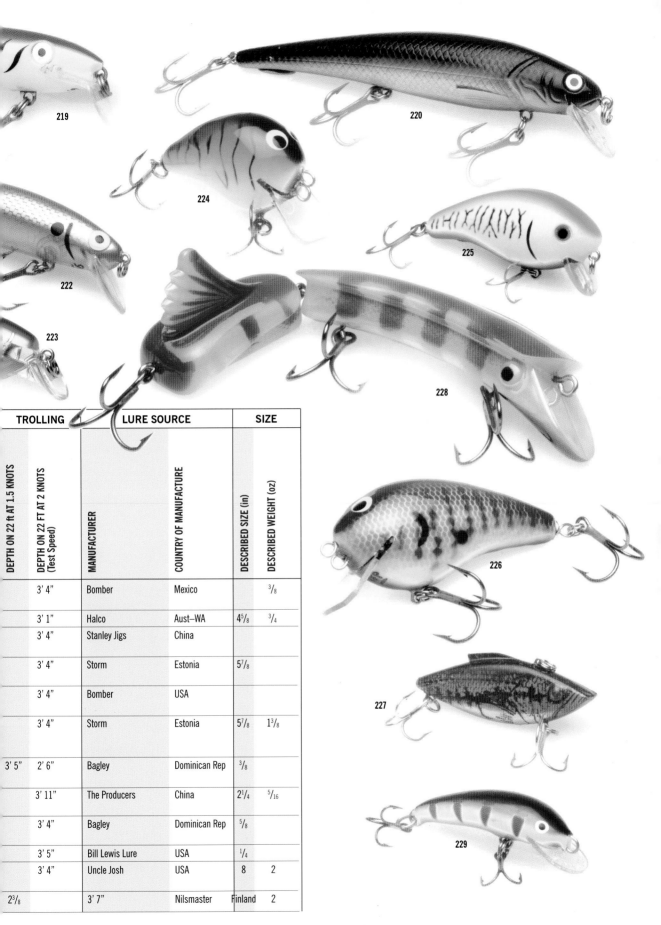

TROLLING		LURE SOURCE		SIZE	
DEPTH ON 22 ft AT 1.5 KNOTS	DEPTH ON 22 FT AT 2 KNOTS (Test Speed)	MANUFACTURER	COUNTRY OF MANUFACTURE	DESCRIBED SIZE (in)	DESCRIBED WEIGHT (oz)
	3' 4"	Bomber	Mexico		$3/8$
	3' 1"	Halco	Aust–WA	$4^5/8$	$3/4$
	3' 4"	Stanley Jigs	China		
	3' 4"	Storm	Estonia	$5^7/8$	
	3' 4"	Bomber	USA		
	3' 4"	Storm	Estonia	$5^7/8$	$1^3/8$
3' 5"	2' 6"	Bagley	Dominican Rep	$3/8$	
	3' 11"	The Producers	China	$2^1/4$	$5/16$
	3' 4"	Bagley	Dominican Rep	$5/8$	
	3' 5"	Bill Lewis Lure	USA	$1/4$	
	3' 4"	Uncle Josh	USA	8	2
$2^3/8$	3' 7"	Nilsmaster	Finland		2

NUMBER	LURE	DEPTH		ACTION		LURE PHYSICAL CHARACTERISTICS							
		DEPTH (FT) ON 66 FT	MAKER'S STATED DEPTH	ACTION	COMMENTS	FLOATING – SINKING – SUSPENDING	BODY MATERIAL PLASTIC – METAL – WOOD – RUBBER	BIB MATERIAL	WIDTH OF BIB (in)	TOW POINT	ACTUAL WEIGHT (oz)	ACTUAL BODY LENGTH (in)	LENGTH WITH BIB (in)
230	MicroMin - Shallow	8' 6"	5'	Tight sway	Great trout lure.	S	P	Plastic	0.31	Nose	$1/8$	$1 5/8$	2
231	Wee Crawfish	8' 6"	4'–6'	Medium sway		F	P	Plastic	0.71	Bib	$3/16$	2	$2 1/2$
232	Bumble Bug	8' 6"	2'	Tight sway	Good action.	F	P	Plastic	0.55	Nose	$3/32$	$1 3/8$	$1 7/8$
233	Husky Jerk HJ12	8' 6"		Slow roll		Sus	P	Plastic	0.56	Nose	$1/2$	$4 5/8$	$4 7/8$
234	A-Salt	8' 6"		Slow roll	Much better faster.		P	Plastic	0.60	Nose	$7/8$	$5 3/4$	$6 3/8$
235	Shakespeare Minnow	8' 6"		Med. sway, medium roll	Great action.		P	Plastic	0.48	Nose	$1 1/4$	5	$5 1/2$
236	Thunderstick	8' 6"	1'–5'	Slow shimmy	Great trolling or casting minnow		P	Plastic	0.57	Nose	$1/4$	$3 1/2$	$3 3/4$
237	Thunderstick 11	8' 6"	2'–5'	Slow sway	Larger minnow		P	Plastic	0.59	Nose	$1/2$	$4 1/2$	$4 7/8$
238	Saltwater Thunderstick	8' 6"	3'–6'	Tight sway, medium roll	Better hardware for tougher fish		P	Plastic	0.57	Nose	$5/8$	$4 1/2$	$4 3/4$
239	Long A H-Duty 7/8oz	8' 6"		Tight roll			P	Plastic	0.58	Nose	$1 1/8$	6	$6 3/8$
240	Prospector 3"	8' 6"		Tight sway	Good action.		R	Plastic	0.57	Nose	$1/2$	$2 3/4$	3
241	Long A Magnum 1 1/2oz	8' 6"		Medium roll			P	Plastic	0.63	Nose	$1 1/2$	7	$7 5/8$
242	Piglet	8' 9"	1'–4'	Slow wide sway—little action	Little action.	F	W	Bibless		Nose	$1 1/8$	$4 3/4$	$5 1/4$

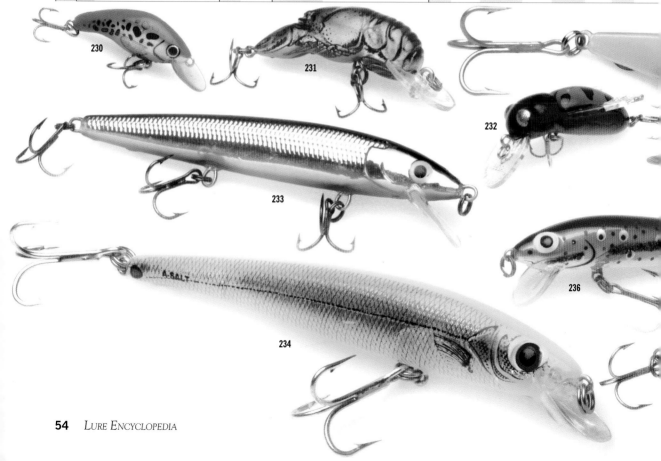

230 231 232 233 234 236

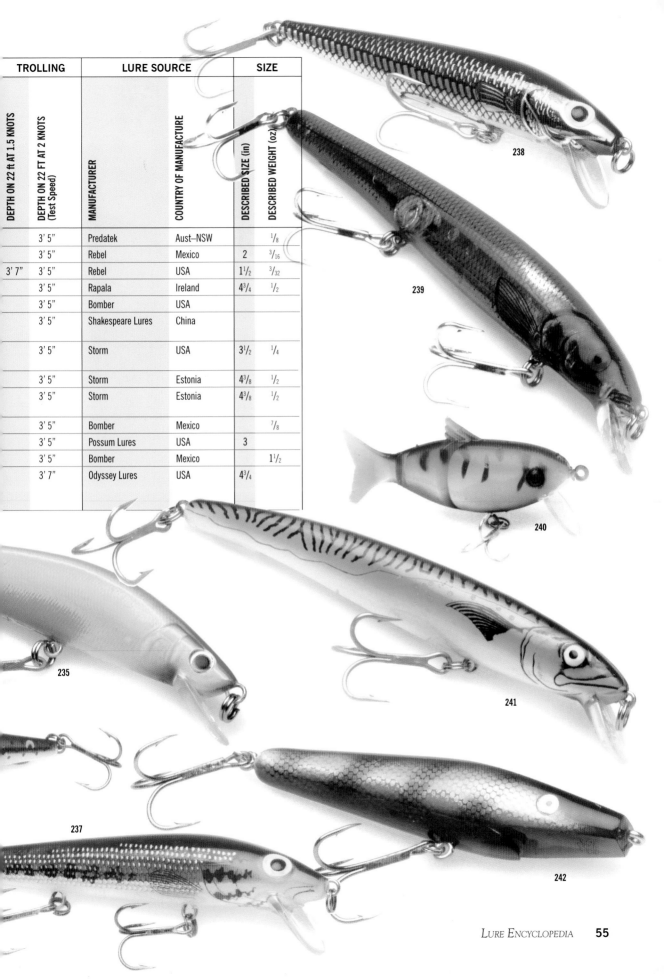

TROLLING		LURE SOURCE		SIZE	
DEPTH ON 22 ft AT 1.5 KNOTS	DEPTH ON 22 FT AT 2 KNOTS (Test Speed)	MANUFACTURER	COUNTRY OF MANUFACTURE	DESCRIBED SIZE (in)	DESCRIBED WEIGHT (oz)
	3' 5"	Predatek	Aust–NSW		$^1/_8$
	3' 5"	Rebel	Mexico	2	$^3/_{16}$
3' 7"	3' 5"	Rebel	USA	$1^1/_2$	$^3/_{32}$
	3' 5"	Rapala	Ireland	$4^3/_4$	$^1/_2$
	3' 5"	Bomber	USA		
	3' 5"	Shakespeare Lures	China		
	3' 5"	Storm	USA	$3^1/_2$	$^1/_4$
	3' 5"	Storm	Estonia	$4^3/_8$	$^1/_2$
	3' 5"	Storm	Estonia	$4^3/_8$	$^1/_2$
	3' 5"	Bomber	Mexico		$^7/_8$
	3' 5"	Possum Lures	USA	3	
	3' 5"	Bomber	Mexico		$1^1/_2$
	3' 7"	Odyssey Lures	USA	$4^3/_4$	

238

239

240

235

241

237

242

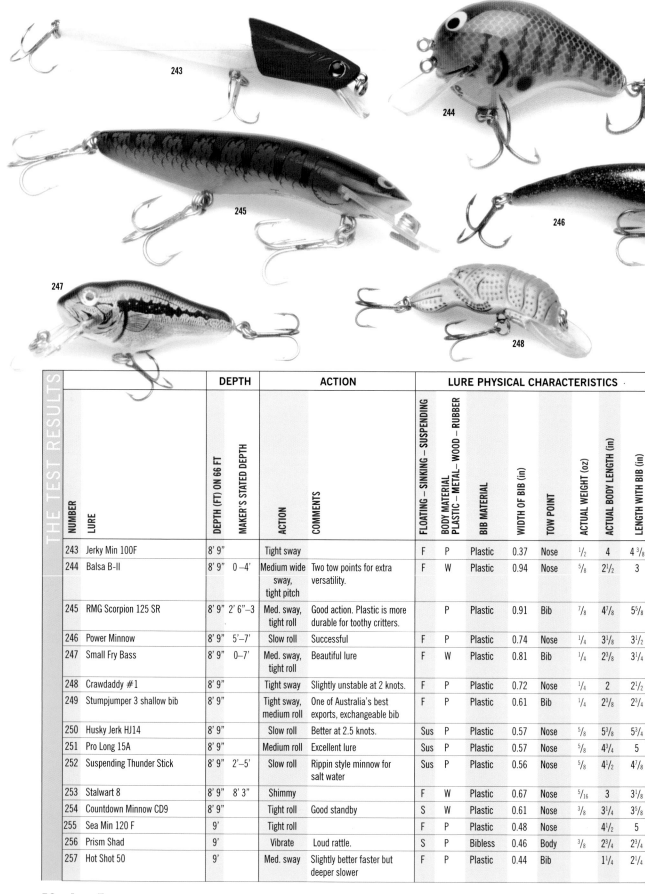

NUMBER	LURE	DEPTH (FT) ON 66 FT	MAKER'S STATED DEPTH	ACTION	COMMENTS	FLOATING – SINKING – SUSPENDING	BODY MATERIAL PLASTIC – METAL – WOOD – RUBBER	BIB MATERIAL	WIDTH OF BIB (in)	TOW POINT	ACTUAL WEIGHT (oz)	ACTUAL BODY LENGTH (in)	LENGTH WITH BIB (in)
243	Jerky Min 100F	8' 9"		Tight sway		F	P	Plastic	0.37	Nose	$^{1}/_{2}$	4	$4\,^{3}/_{8}$
244	Balsa B-II	8' 9"	0 –4'	Medium wide sway, tight pitch	Two tow points for extra versatility.	F	W	Plastic	0.94	Nose	$^{5}/_{8}$	$2\,^{1}/_{2}$	3
245	RMG Scorpion 125 SR	8' 9"	2' 6"–3	Med. sway, tight roll	Good action. Plastic is more durable for toothy critters.		P	Plastic	0.91	Bib	$^{7}/_{8}$	$4\,^{7}/_{8}$	$5\,^{5}/_{8}$
246	Power Minnow	8' 9"	5'–7'	Slow roll	Successful	F	P	Plastic	0.74	Nose	$^{1}/_{4}$	$3\,^{1}/_{8}$	$3\,^{1}/_{2}$
247	Small Fry Bass	8' 9"	0–7'	Med. sway, tight roll	Beautiful lure	F	W	Plastic	0.81	Bib	$^{1}/_{4}$	$2\,^{3}/_{8}$	$3\,^{1}/_{4}$
248	Crawdaddy #1	8' 9"		Tight sway	Slightly unstable at 2 knots.	F	P	Plastic	0.72	Nose	$^{1}/_{4}$	2	$2\,^{1}/_{2}$
249	Stumpjumper 3 shallow bib	8' 9"		Tight sway, medium roll	One of Australia's best exports, exchangeable bib	F	P	Plastic	0.61	Bib	$^{1}/_{4}$	$2\,^{3}/_{8}$	$2\,^{3}/_{4}$
250	Husky Jerk HJ14	8' 9"		Slow roll	Better at 2.5 knots.	Sus	P	Plastic	0.57	Nose	$^{5}/_{8}$	$5\,^{3}/_{8}$	$5\,^{3}/_{8}$
251	Pro Long 15A	8' 9"		Medium roll	Excellent lure	Sus	P	Plastic	0.57	Nose	$^{5}/_{8}$	$4\,^{3}/_{4}$	5
252	Suspending Thunder Stick	8' 9"	2'–5'	Slow roll	Rippin style minnow for salt water	Sus	P	Plastic	0.56	Nose	$^{5}/_{8}$	$4\,^{1}/_{2}$	$4\,^{7}/_{8}$
253	Stalwart 8	8' 9"	8' 3"	Shimmy		F	W	Plastic	0.67	Nose	$^{5}/_{16}$	3	$3\,^{1}/_{8}$
254	Countdown Minnow CD9	8' 9"		Tight roll	Good standby	S	W	Plastic	0.61	Nose	$^{3}/_{8}$	$3\,^{1}/_{4}$	$3\,^{5}/_{8}$
255	Sea Min 120 F	9'		Tight roll		F	P	Plastic	0.48	Nose		$4\,^{1}/_{2}$	5
256	Prism Shad	9'		Vibrate	Loud rattle.	S	P	Bibless	0.46	Body	$^{3}/_{8}$	$2\,^{3}/_{4}$	$2\,^{3}/_{4}$
257	Hot Shot 50	9'		Med. sway	Slightly better faster but deeper slower	F	P	Plastic	0.44	Bib		$1\,^{1}/_{4}$	$2\,^{1}/_{4}$

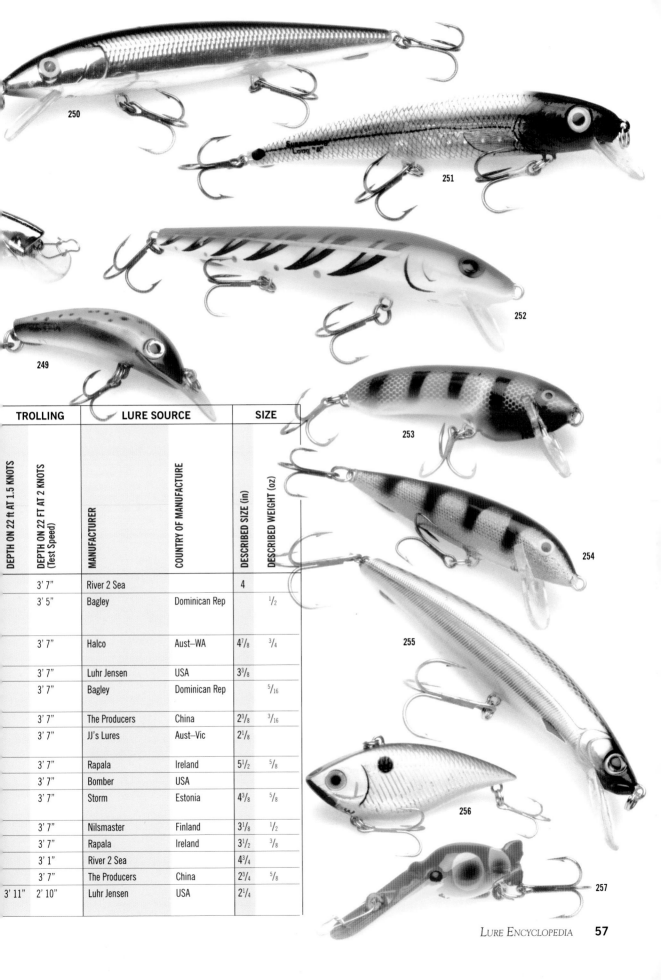

TROLLING		LURE SOURCE		SIZE	
DEPTH ON 22 ft AT 1.5 KNOTS	DEPTH ON 22 FT AT 2 KNOTS (Test Speed)	MANUFACTURER	COUNTRY OF MANUFACTURE	DESCRIBED SIZE (in)	DESCRIBED WEIGHT (oz)
	3' 7"	River 2 Sea		4	
	3' 5"	Bagley	Dominican Rep		$1/2$
	3' 7"	Halco	Aust—WA	$4^7/_8$	$3/_4$
	3' 7"	Luhr Jensen	USA	$3^3/_8$	
	3' 7"	Bagley	Dominican Rep		$5/_{16}$
	3' 7"	The Producers	China	$2^3/_8$	$3/_{16}$
	3' 7"	JJ's Lures	Aust—Vic	$2^1/_8$	
	3' 7"	Rapala	Ireland	$5^1/_2$	$5/_8$
	3' 7"	Bomber	USA		
	3' 7"	Storm	Estonia	$4^3/_8$	$5/_8$
	3' 7"	Nilsmaster	Finland	$3^1/_8$	$1/_2$
	3' 7"	Rapala	Ireland	$3^1/_2$	$3/_8$
	3' 1"	River 2 Sea		$4^3/_4$	
	3' 7"	The Producers	China	$2^3/_4$	$5/_8$
3' 11"	2' 10"	Luhr Jensen	USA	$2^1/_4$	

| NUMBER | LURE | DEPTH | | ACTION | | LURE PHYSICAL CHARACTERISTICS | | | | | | | | |
		DEPTH (FT) ON 66 FT	MAKER'S STATED DEPTH	ACTION	COMMENTS	FLOATING – SINKING – SUSPENDING	BODY MATERIAL PLASTIC – METAL– WOOD – RUBBER	BIB MATERIAL	WIDTH OF BIB (in)	TOW POINT	ACTUAL WEIGHT (oz)	ACTUAL BODY LENGTH (in)	LENGTH WITH BIB (in)
258	Clancy's Dancer No 4	9' 3"		Tight sway		F	P	Plastic	0.61	Bib	$1/4$	$3^3/8$	$4^1/2$
259	X 4 Flatfish	9' 3"		Wide sway	Better at 1.5 knots.	F	P	Plastic	0.69	Body	$3/16$	$1^7/8$	$2^3/4$
260	Mad N	9' 3"	4'	Tight sway	Good Norman lure		P	Plastic	0.80	Bib	$5/16$	2	$2^3/4$
261	Shad Rap Shallow 9	9' 3"		Shimmy		F	W	Plastic	0.70	Nose	$3/8$	$3^3/4$	$4^1/4$
262	Invincible 12	9' 3"	6' 6"	Slow medium roll	Versatile and hugely successful	F	W	Plastic	0.67	Nose	$3/4$	$4^1/2$	5
263	Husky Jerk 10 Suspending	9' 3"	4'–8'	Tight sway, tight roll	Great rippin' lure	Sus	P	Plastic	0.56	Nose	$5/16$	$3^3/4$	$4^1/8$
264	Spearhead 8	9' 3"	8' 3"	Tight sway		F	W	Plastic	0.67	Nose	$3/8$	$2^7/8$	$3^1/4$
265	Husky Jerk Susp 14	9' 3"		Slow roll	Suspending in larger lure	Sus	P	Plastic	0.57	Nose	$5/8$	$5^3/8$	$5^3/4$
266	Spence Scout	9' 3"		Tight sway	Great action.	F	P	Metal	0.70	Nose	$1/2$	$2^3/8$	$2^3/4$
267	Surfi Vib 80	9' 6"		Vibrate	Heavy sinking lure	S	P	Bibless		Body		$3^1/8$	$3^1/8$
268	Invincible 12J	9' 6"	6' 6"	Shimmy, tight pitch		F	W	Plastic	0.67	Nose	$3/4$	$4^3/4$	$5^1/4$
269	Big Z	9' 6"		Tight sway, slow roll		F	P	Plastic	0.85	Nose	$5/8$	3	$3^1/2$
270	Midive Min 80F	9' 6"		Med. sway, tight roll	Very good lure	F	P	Plastic	0.55	Bib	$5/16$	$3^1/8$	$3^7/8$

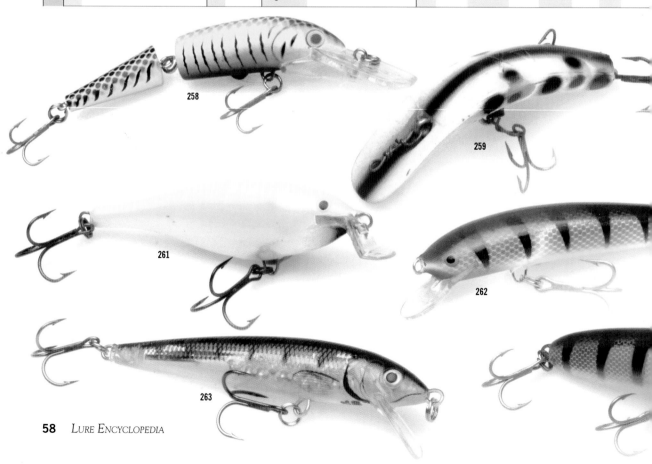

258

261

263

259

262

TROLLING		LURE SOURCE		SIZE	
DEPTH ON 22 ft AT 1.5 KNOTS	DEPTH ON 22 FT AT 2 KNOTS (Test Speed)	MANUFACTURER	COUNTRY OF MANUFACTURE	DESCRIBED SIZE (in)	DESCRIBED WEIGHT (oz)
	3' 5"	The Producers	China	$3^1/_4$	$^1/_4$
3' 9"	3' 7"	Worden's	USA		
	3' 10"	Norman Lures	USA		$^3/_8$
	3' 10"	Rapala	Finland	$3^1/_2$	$^3/_8$
	3' 10"	Nilsmaster	Finland	$4^3/_4$	$^7/_8$
	3' 10"	Rapala	Ireland	$3^7/_8$	$^3/_8$
	3' 10"	Nilsmaster	Finland	$3^1/_8$	$^1/_2$
	3' 10"	Rapala	Ireland	$5^1/_2$	$^5/_8$
	3' 10"	Strike King Lure Co.	Costa Rica		
	3' 10"	River 2 Sea		$3^1/_8$	
	4'	Nilsmaster	Finland	$4^3/_4$	$^7/_8$
	3' 10"	The Producers	China	$3^1/_2$	$^5/_8$
	3' 7"	River 2 Sea		$3^1/_8$	

267

268

269

260

270

265

264

266

271

273

272

277

276

278

		DEPTH		ACTION		LURE PHYSICAL CHARACTERISTICS							
NUMBER	LURE	DEPTH (FT) ON 66 FT	MAKER'S STATED DEPTH	ACTION	COMMENTS	FLOATING – SINKING – SUSPENDING	BODY MATERIAL PLASTIC – METAL– WOOD – RUBBER	BIB MATERIAL	WIDTH OF BIB (in)	TOW POINT	ACTUAL WEIGHT (oz)	ACTUAL BODY LENGTH (in)	LENGTH WITH BIB (in)
271	Super Spot	9' 6"		Tight sway, vibrate	Loud rattle.	S	P	Bibless	0.39	Body	$5/16$	$2^1/2$	$2^1/2$
272	Suspending Super Rogue	9' 9"	5'	Tight pitch	Slightly better at 2.5 knot	Sus	P	Plastic	0.65	Nose	$1/2$	$4^7/8$	$5^1/4$
273	Diver Vib 65	9' 9"		Needs speed	Needs at least 2.5 knots.	S	P	Bibless		Body	$7/8$	$2^1/2$	$2^5/8$
274	Super Spot	9' 9"		Tight sway, vibrate	Great action. Best action of rattling type lures. Better at 2 knots.	S	P	Bibless		Body	$1/2$	3	3
275	Trembler 70	9' 9"	2' 3"	Vibrate	Much better faster but this Trembler can work at slow speeds.	S	P	Bibless	0.50	Body	$5/8$	$2^3/4$	$2^3/4$
276	Elmo's Zipfish #6	9' 9"		Wide sway	Needs 1.5 knots or slower.	F	P	Plastic	1.06	Body	$5/8$	$3^1/8$	$4^1/2$
277	RMG Scorpion 52 STD	9' 9"	5' 3"	Tight roll	One of Australia's best		P	Plastic	0.63	Nose	$3/16$	$2^1/4$	$2^3/4$
278	Klawdad	10'		Shimmy	Popular	F	P	Plastic	0.69	Bib	$1/4$	$2^1/4$	$2^3/4$
279	RMG Scorpion 52 DD	10'	8' 3"	Tight sway, tight roll	Great action. Many applications		P	Plastic	0.66	Bib	$3/16$	$2^1/4$	$3^1/8$
280	Baby 4-	10'	4'	Med. sway, tight roll	Nice action and appearance		P	Plastic	0.87	Nose	$3/8$	$2^1/4$	$2^5/8$
281	Tail Dancer TD7	10'		Tight sway, tight roll	Nice finish		W	Plastic	0.67	Bib	$5/16$	$2^7/8$	4
282	Premier Pro-Model Series 1	10'	2'–5'	Med. sway		F	P	Plastic	0.82	Nose	$5/16$	2	$2^5/8$
283	Deep Tiny N	10'	4'–6'	Tight sway			P	Plastic	0.59	Bib	$3/16$	$1^5/8$	$2^1/2$
284	Model 2A	10'		Tight sway, tight pitch	Quality favorite		P	Plastic	0.72	Bib	$5/16$	$2^1/8$	$2^5/8$

THE TEST RESULTS

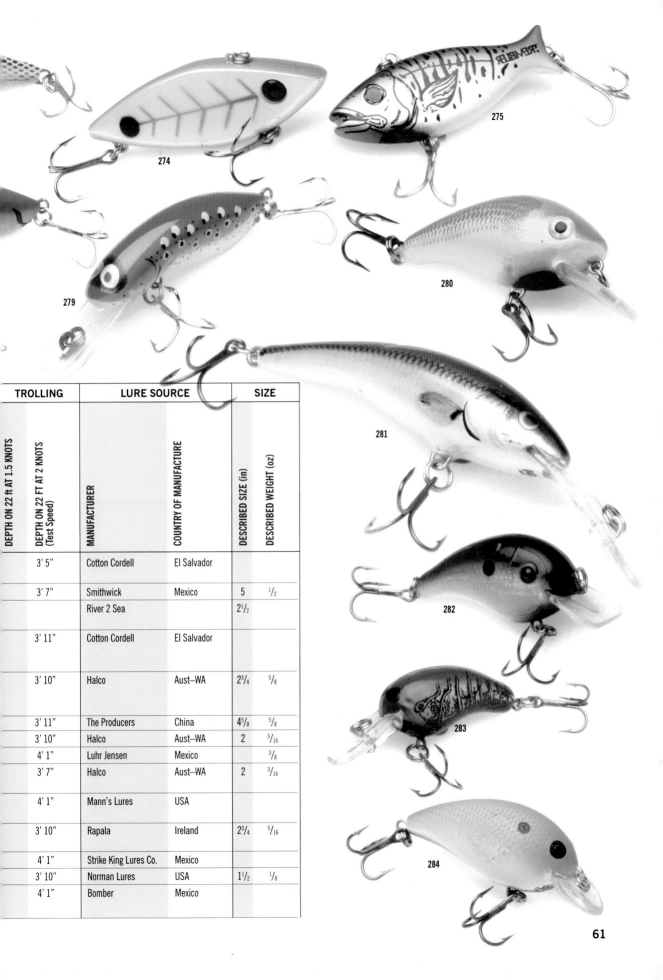

TROLLING		LURE SOURCE		SIZE	
DEPTH ON 22 ft AT 1.5 KNOTS	DEPTH ON 22 FT AT 2 KNOTS (Test Speed)	MANUFACTURER	COUNTRY OF MANUFACTURE	DESCRIBED SIZE (in)	DESCRIBED WEIGHT (oz)
	3' 5"	Cotton Cordell	El Salvador		
	3' 7"	Smithwick	Mexico	5	$1/2$
		River 2 Sea		$2^1/2$	
	3' 11"	Cotton Cordell	El Salvador		
	3' 10"	Halco	Aust—WA	$2^3/4$	$5/8$
	3' 11"	The Producers	China	$4^5/8$	$5/8$
	3' 10"	Halco	Aust—WA	2	$3/16$
	4' 1"	Luhr Jensen	Mexico		$3/8$
	3' 7"	Halco	Aust—WA	2	$3/16$
	4' 1"	Mann's Lures	USA		
	3' 10"	Rapala	Ireland	$2^3/4$	$5/16$
	4' 1"	Strike King Lures Co.	Mexico		
	3' 10"	Norman Lures	USA	$1^1/2$	$1/8$
	4' 1"	Bomber	Mexico		

61

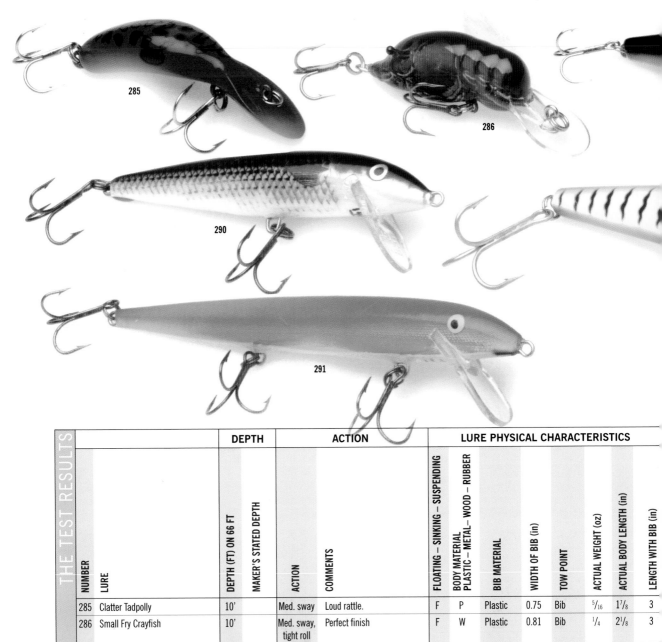

THE TEST RESULTS	NUMBER	LURE	DEPTH		ACTION		LURE PHYSICAL CHARACTERISTICS							
			DEPTH (FT) ON 66 FT	MAKER'S STATED DEPTH	ACTION	COMMENTS	FLOATING – SINKING – SUSPENDING	BODY MATERIAL PLASTIC – METAL – WOOD – RUBBER	BIB MATERIAL	WIDTH OF BIB (in)	TOW POINT	ACTUAL WEIGHT (oz)	ACTUAL BODY LENGTH (in)	LENGTH WITH BIB (in)
	285	Clatter Tadpolly	10'		Med. sway	Loud rattle.	F	P	Plastic	0.75	Bib	$^5/_{16}$	$1^7/_8$	3
	286	Small Fry Crayfish	10'		Med. sway, tight roll	Perfect finish	F	W	Plastic	0.81	Bib	$^1/_4$	$2^1/_8$	3
	287	Static Shad 70 Su	10'		Tight sway	Great lure	Sus	P	Plastic	0.60	Bib	$^3/_8$	$2^7/_8$	$3^5/_8$
	288	River Minnow	10'		Med. sway	Prefer others		P	Metal	0.79	Nose	$^1/_4$	$2^1/_4$	$2^5/_8$
	289	MinMin Deep	10'	8' 3"	Tight sway	Great action. Must have	F	P	Plastic	0.66	Bib	$^1/_8$	2	$3^1/_8$
	290	Countdown Minnow CD11	10'		Slow roll		S	W	Plastic	0.70	Nose	$^5/_8$	$4^1/_8$	$4^3/_8$
	291	Original Minnow 18	10' 3"		Tight roll	Old favorite	F	P	Plastic	0.59	Nose	$^3/_4$	$6^1/_2$	$6^7/_8$
	292	Barramundi Mauler 9	10' 3"		Tight sway, wide roll			P	Plastic	1.13	Bib	$1^5/_8$	7	$8^7/_8$
	293	Obese Crank 45	10' 6"		Tight sway	Better at 1.5 knots. Good finish	F	P	Plastic	0.73	Nose	$^3/_8$	$1^3/_4$	$2^1/_4$
	294	Honey B	10' 6"	0–7'	Tight sway	Great action.	F	W	Plastic	0.81	Bib	$^3/_{16}$	$1^1/_2$	$2^1/_2$
	295	Little Z	10' 6"		Tight sway		F	P	Plastic	0.65	Nose	$^1/_2$	$2^5/_8$	$3^1/_4$
	296	MicroMin - Deep	10' 6"	8' 3"	Tight sway	Deep for small lure. Nice finish.	S	P	Plastic	0.66	Bib	$^3/_{32}$	$1^5/_8$	$2^5/_8$
	297	TD Hyper Shad Ti60	10' 6"		Med. sway	Great action.	F	P	Metal	0.73	Bib	$^3/_8$	$2^5/_8$	$3^7/_8$
	298	Magnum Mag-11	10' 6"		Tight sway		F	W	Plastic	0.69	Nose	$^1/_2$	$4^3/_8$	$5^1/_8$

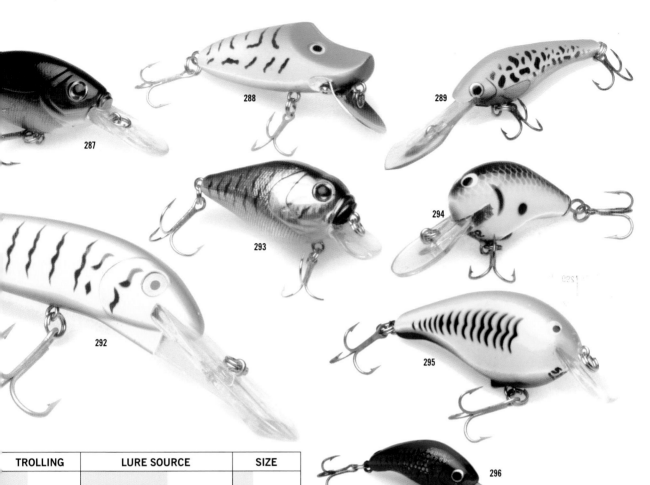

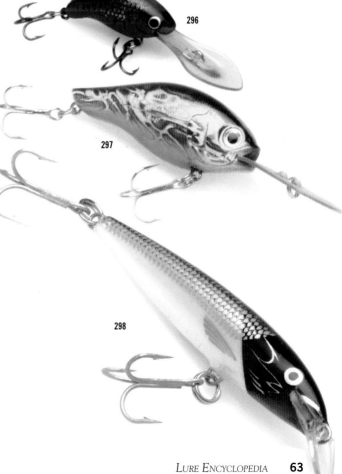

TROLLING		LURE SOURCE		SIZE	
DEPTH ON 22 ft AT 1.5 KNOTS	DEPTH ON 22 FT AT 2 KNOTS (Test Speed)	MANUFACTURER	COUNTRY OF MANUFACTURE	DESCRIBED SIZE (in)	DESCRIBED WEIGHT (oz)
	3' 10"	Heddon	USA		
	4' 1"	Bagley	Dominican Rep		
	3' 10"	River 2 Sea		$2^3/_4$	
	4' 1"	The Producers	China	$2^1/_4$	$1/_4$
	3' 10"	Predatek	Aust–NSW		$1/_8$
	4' 1"	Rapala	Ireland	$4^3/_8$	$5/_8$
	4' 1"	Rapala	Ireland	$7^1/_8$	$3/_4$
	4' 1"	The Producers	China	9	$1^3/_4$
	3' 11"	River 2 Sea		$1^3/_4$	
	4' 4"	Bagley	Dominican Rep		$1/_4$
	4' 4"	The Producers	China	$3^1/_8$	$3/_8$
	3' 11"	Predatek	Aust–NSW		$1/_8$
	3' 11"	Team Diawa	Japan	$2^3/_8$	$3/_8$
	4' 4"	Rapala	Ireland	$4^3/_8$	$1/_2$

NUMBER	LURE	DEPTH (FT) ON 66 FT	MAKER'S STATED DEPTH	ACTION	COMMENTS	FLOATING – SINKING – SUSPENDING	BODY MATERIAL PLASTIC – METAL – WOOD – RUBBER	BIB MATERIAL	WIDTH OF BIB (in)	TOW POINT	ACTUAL WEIGHT (oz)	ACTUAL BODY LENGTH (in)	LENGTH WITH BIB (in)
299	Jointed Minnow J-13	10' 6"		Tight sway, tight pitch		F	P	Plastic	0.67	Nose	$^5/_8$	5	$5^7/_8$
300	TD Hyper Minnow 90	10' 6"		Medium roll	Great fish catcher	F	P	Metal	0.74	Bib	$^3/_8$	$3^1/_2$	$4^3/_4$
301	Rat-L-Trap Rattletrap	10' 6"		Tight sway	Even better with spinner blade added	S	P	Bibless	0.38	Body	$^5/_8$	3	3
302	Zero #3	10' 6"		Vibrate		S	P	Bibless	0.41	Body	$^5/_8$	3	3
303	Rattlin' Rapala RNR7	10' 6"		Shimmy		S	P	Bibless	0.48	Body	$^1/_2$	$2^7/_8$	3
304	Big O 1/4 oz	10' 9"		Tight sway			P	Plastic	0.61	Nose	$^1/_4$	2	$2^1/_2$
305	RMG Scorpion 68 STD	11'	8' 3"	Tight sway	Many applications		P	Plastic	0.86	Bib	$^5/_{16}$	$2^3/_4$	$3^1/_2$
306	Jindivik	11'		Tight sway, medium roll	Unique bib design high quality	F	P	Plastic	1.14	Bib	$^5/_8$	$3^1/_4$	$4^1/_4$
307	Shad Rap Deep SR5	11'		Fast sway	Must have lure	F	W	Plastic	0.61	Bib	$^3/_{16}$	$2^1/_4$	$3^1/_8$
308	Premier Pro-Model Series 4S	11'	2'–4'	Med. sway, tight roll	High quality		P	Plastic	0.90	Nose	$^5/_8$	$2^1/_2$	$3^1/_8$
309	Slavko Bug - Oh Bug	11'	5'	Tight sway	Fantastic lure hard to get	F	P	Plastic	0.64	Bib	$^1/_8$	$2^1/_8$	$3^1/_8$
310	Invincible DR8	11'	10'	Tight roll			W	Plastic	0.66	Nose	$^1/_4$	$2^7/_8$	$3^3/_8$
311	Avoidance Behaviour Lure - Eel	11'		Med. wide sway	Excellent action but must be at 1.5 knots.	F	P	Plastic	0.86	Bib	$^3/_8$	2	$3^7/_8$

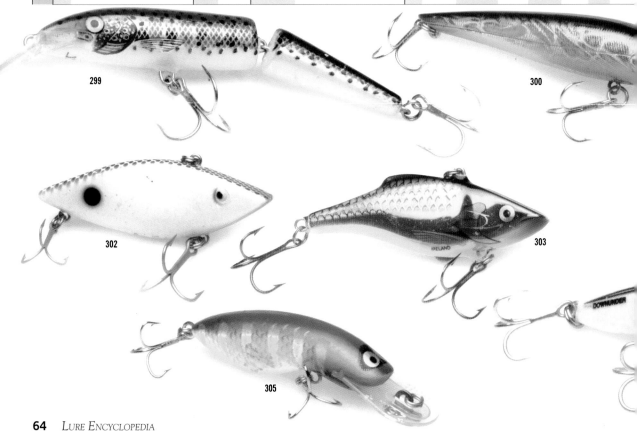

299 300 302 303 305

| TROLLING | | LURE SOURCE | | SIZE | |
DEPTH ON 22 ft AT 1.5 KNOTS	DEPTH ON 22 FT AT 2 KNOTS (Test Speed)	MANUFACTURER	COUNTRY OF MANUFACTURE	DESCRIBED SIZE (in)	DESCRIBED WEIGHT (oz)
4' 4"		Rapala	Ireland	$5\frac{1}{8}$	$\frac{5}{8}$
4'		Team Diawa	Japan	$3\frac{4}{8}$	$\frac{3}{8}$
4' 1"		Bill Lewis Lures	USA		$\frac{1}{2}$
3' 11"		The Producers	China	3	$\frac{1}{2}$
4' 1"		Rapala	Ireland	$2\frac{3}{4}$	$\frac{5}{8}$
4' 1"		Cotton Cordell	El Salvador		
4' 1"		Halco	Aust–WA	$2\frac{5}{8}$	$\frac{1}{4}$
4' 1"		Predatek	Aust–NSW		
4' 1"		Rapala	Ireland	2	$\frac{3}{16}$
4' 5"		Strike King Lures Co.	Mexico		
4' 1"		Yo-Zuri Lures	Japan	$2\frac{1}{8}$	$\frac{3}{16}$
4' 4"		Nilsmaster	Finland	$3\frac{1}{8}$	$\frac{1}{4}$
4' 4"	0.0	Bass Pro Shops	China		

308

309

310

301

311

304

306

307

		DEPTH		ACTION		LURE PHYSICAL CHARACTERISTICS							
NUMBER	LURE	DEPTH (FT) ON 66 FT	MAKER'S STATED DEPTH	ACTION	COMMENTS	FLOATING – SINKING – SUSPENDING	BODY MATERIAL PLASTIC – METAL – WOOD – RUBBER	BIB MATERIAL	WIDTH OF BIB (in)	TOW POINT	ACTUAL WEIGHT (oz)	ACTUAL BODY LENGTH (in)	LENGTH WITH BIB (in)
312	Clancy's Dancer No 5	11'		Medium roll			P	Plastic	0.87	Bib	$^1/_2$	$4^3/_8$	$5^5/_8$
313	Mid Wart	11' 3" 8' 3"–1		Med. sway	Good trolling and casting performance		P	Plastic	0.80	Bib	$^5/_{16}$	2	$2^5/_8$
314	Kill'r B-I	11' 3" 0–7'		Tight sway		F	W	Plastic	0.81	Bib	$^5/_{16}$	$1^7/_8$	$2^3/_4$
315	Stretch 5+	11' 3" 5'		Tight sway	Great action. Extremely popular	P	Plastic		0.77	Bib	$^1/_4$	$2^1/_2$	$3^3/_4$
316	Rattlin' Rapala RNR8	11' 3"		Vibrate		S	P	Bibless	0.51	Body	$^3/_4$	$3^3/_8$	$3^3/_8$
317	Tadpolly	11' 6"		Med. sway	Old classic	F	P	Plastic	0.75	Bib	$^5/_{16}$	$1^7/_8$	3
318	5+	11' 6" 5'		Tight sway	Much better at 1.5 knots. Top lure		P	Plastic	0.80	Bib	$^3/_{16}$	$1^5/_8$	$2^1/_2$
319	Clawdaddy #2	11' 6"		Med. sway	Great deep crayfish lure	F	P	Plastic	0.90	Bib	$^5/_{16}$	$2^1/_4$	$3^1/_4$
320	Mimic Series 80	11' 6"		No action— not for trolling	Rippin' minnow. Needs lots of work		P	Plastic	0.63	Nose	$^1/_2$	$3^1/_8$	$3^3/_4$
321	Laser Pro 120 DD	11' 6" 6' 6"		Med. sway	Saltwater standby		P	Plastic	0.73	Nose	$^5/_8$	$4^5/_8$	$5^3/_8$
322	Deep ThunderStick	11' 6" 8'–12'		Med. sway, medium roll	Good action.		P	Plastic	0.69	Bib	$^5/_{16}$	$3^1/_2$	$4^5/_8$
323	Prism Shad #3S	11' 6"		Vibrate		S	P	Bibless	0.46	Body	$^3/_4$	$3^3/_8$	$3^3/_8$
324	Mud Bug 1/8oz	11' 6"		Med. sway, tight pitch	Catches fish very well	F	P	Metal	0.79	Bib	$^1/_4$	$1^1/_2$	$2^3/_4$
325	Diver Vib 80	11' 6"		Needs speed	Needs at least 2.5 knots.	S	P	Bibless		Body	$1^1/_2$	$3^1/_8$	$3^1/_4$

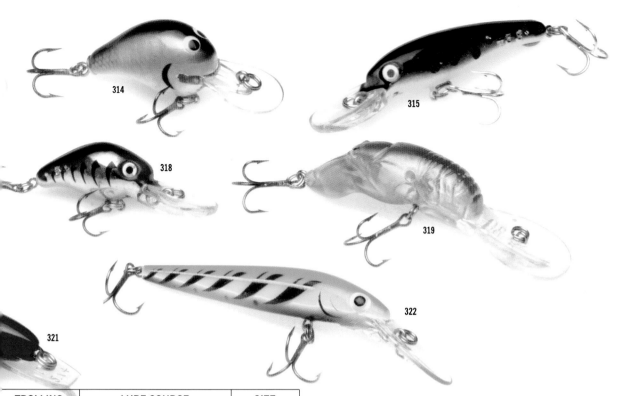

314

315

318

319

322

321

323

324

325

TROLLING		LURE SOURCE		SIZE	
DEPTH ON 22 ft AT 1.5 KNOTS	DEPTH ON 22 FT AT 2 KNOTS (Test Speed)	MANUFACTURER	COUNTRY OF MANUFACTURE	DESCRIBED SIZE (in)	DESCRIBED WEIGHT (oz)
	4' 5"	The Producers	China	$5^1/_2$	$^1/_2$
	4' 4"	Storm	Estonia	2	$^5/_{16}$
	4' 5"	Bagley	Dominican Rep		$^5/_{16}$
	4' 4"	Mann's Lures	USA		
	4' 4"	Rapala	Ireland	$3^1/_8$	$^3/_4$
	4' 4"	Heddon	USA		
4' 7"	4' 4"	Mann's Lures	USA		$^3/_{32}$
	4' 4"	The Producers	China	$3^3/_8$	$^1/_4$
	4' 4"	Saiko Lures	China		
	4' 4"	Halco	Aust–WA	$4^5/_8$	$^3/_4$
	4' 4"	Storm	Estonia	$3^1/_2$	$^5/_{16}$
	4' 4"	The Producers	China	$3^3/_8$	$^3/_4$
	4' 7"	Fred Arbogast	USA		$^1/_8$
		River 2 Sea		$3^1/_8$	

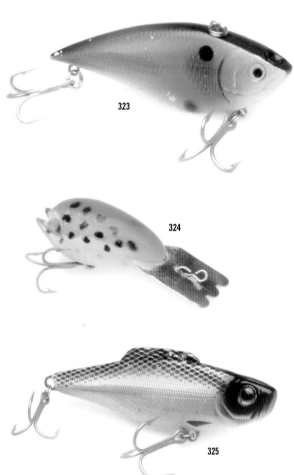

NUMBER	LURE	DEPTH (FT) ON 66 FT	MAKER'S STATED DEPTH	ACTION	COMMENTS	FLOATING – SINKING – SUSPENDING	BODY MATERIAL PLASTIC – METAL – WOOD – RUBBER	BIB MATERIAL	WIDTH OF BIB (in)	TOW POINT	ACTUAL WEIGHT (oz)	ACTUAL BODY LENGTH (in)	LENGTH WITH BIB (in)
326	Mohican Dart	11' 9"		Tight sway	Unusual makers		W	Metal	0.71	Bib	$5/16$	$2^3/8$	$3^1/4$
327	Fastrac Jointed FTJ20	11' 9"	11' 6"	Tight sway		F	P	Plastic	0.76	Bib	$1/2$	$4^5/8$	$5^1/2$
328	Midi S	11' 9"		Med. sway	Old favorite		P	Plastic	0.77	Nose	$1/2$	$2^3/8$	3
329	RMG Scorpion 68 DD	11' 9"	10'	Tight sway, slow roll	Need to have one		P	Plastic	0.88	Bib	$5/16$	$2^3/4$	$3^7/8$
330	Model 5A	11' 9"		Tight sway	Lateral movement.		P	Plastic	0.70	Bib	$1/4$	$1^3/4$	$2^5/8$
331	Magnum CD-7	11' 9"		Medium roll	Better faster. Takes all fish.	S	W	Metal	0.59	Bib	$3/8$	$2^7/8$	$3^3/4$
332	Invincible 18	11' 9"		Medium roll	Better at 2.5 knots.		W	Plastic	0.89	Nose	$1^5/8$	$7^1/8$	$7^5/8$
333	Static Shad 60 Su	11' 9"		Tight sway, tight pitch		Sus	P	Plastic	0.59	Bib	$3/16$	$2^1/4$	$3^1/8$
334	Tail Dancer TD9	11' 9"	6' 3"–11' 6"	Med. sway, medium roll	Great action.		W	Plastic	0.76	Bib	$1/2$	$3^1/2$	$4^3/4$
335	Sliver Jointed 13	11' 9"		Tight sway, medium roll	Great action at 2.5 knots.		P	Metal	0.55	Bib		$5^3/8$	$6^1/2$
336	Fat Rap FR5	12'		Fast sway	A must have lure	F	W	Plastic	0.71	Bib	$3/8$	$2^1/8$	3
337	Double Downer #2	12'		Med. sway	Better at 1.5 knots.		P	Metal	0.87	Bib	$1/4$	2	3
338	Crawdad	12'	7'	Med. sway, tight roll	Loud rattle.		P	Plastic	0.78	Bib	$3/8$	$2^1/8$	$3^1/8$
339	Jointed Pikie 3000	12'	4'–7' casting 9'–12' trolling	Tight sway	Little action.	S	P	Metal	1.06	Bib	$1^1/2$	$5^7/8$	$6^7/8$

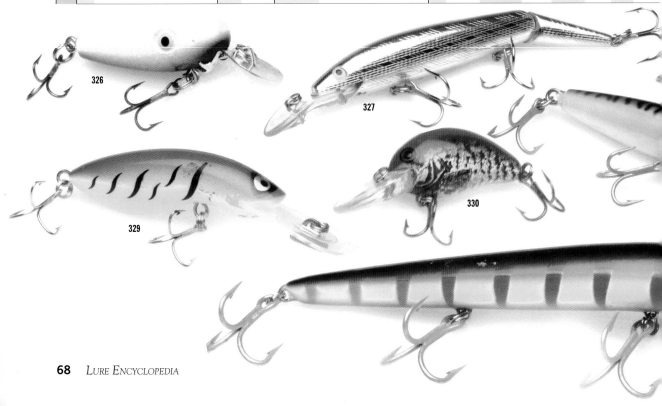

326

327

329

330

TROLLING		LURE SOURCE		SIZE	
DEPTH ON 22 ft AT 1.5 KNOTS	DEPTH ON 22 FT AT 2 KNOTS (Test Speed)	MANUFACTURER	COUNTRY OF MANUFACTURE	DESCRIBED SIZE (in)	DESCRIBED WEIGHT (oz)
	4' 5"	Dream Catcher Lures	USA		$5/16$
	4' 5"	Rebel	USA	$4\frac{1}{2}$	$3/8$
	4' 5"	Shakespeare Lures			
	4' 5"	Halco	Aust—WA	$2\frac{5}{8}$	$1/4$
	4' 5"	Bomber	Mexico		
	4' 5"	Rapala	Estonia	$2\frac{3}{4}$	$3/8$
	4' 5"	Nilsmaster	Finland	$7\frac{1}{8}$	$1\frac{3}{8}$
	4' 5"	River 2 Sea		$2\frac{3}{8}$	
	4' 5"	Rapala	Ireland	$3\frac{4}{8}$	$1/2$
	4' 5"	Rapala	Ireland	$5\frac{1}{8}$	$5/8$
	4' 7"	Rapala	Ireland	2	$1/4$
4' 7"	4' 5"	The Producers	China	3	$1/4$
	4' 7"	Mann's Lures	USA		$1/4$
	4' 9"	Creek Chub	El Salvador	6	$1\frac{3}{4}$

333

334

335

336

328

337

338

332

339

340

TREMBLER 341

345

344

		DEPTH		ACTION		LURE PHYSICAL CHARACTERISTICS								
NUMBER	LURE	DEPTH (FT) ON 66 FT	MAKER'S STATED DEPTH	ACTION	COMMENTS	FLOATING – SINKING – SUSPENDING	BODY MATERIAL PLASTIC – METAL– WOOD – RUBBER	BIB MATERIAL	WIDTH OF BIB (in)	TOW POINT	ACTUAL WEIGHT (oz)	ACTUAL BODY LENGTH (in)	LENGTH WITH BIB (in)
340	Magnum Stretch 8+	12'	8'	Med. sway, wide roll	Better at 2.5 knots and much more.		P	Plastic	1.44	Bib	$3^1/_2$	$8^1/_2$	10
341	Trembler 110	12'	3' 4"	Vibrate	Can run at 8 knots or more	S	P	Bibless	0.62	Body	$1^1/_2$	$4^1/_8$	$4^1/_8$
342	Mud Bug 1/4oz	12'		Med. sway	Erratic lateral movement, but stable.	F	P	Metal	0.92	Bib	$^3/_8$	2	3
343	Tilsan Minnow	12'	8' 3"	Tight roll	Great wooden lure	F	W	Plastic	0.67	Bib	$^3/_{16}$	$2^1/_4$	$3^3/_8$
344	Barramundi Mauler 4	12'		Tight shimmy			P	Plastic	0.68	Bib	$^1/_4$	$3^1/_8$	4
345	RMG Scorpion 125 STD	12' 3"	10'	Tight sway, tight roll	Very good trolling lure		P	Plastic	1.09	Bib	$^7/_8$	$4^7/_8$	$5^7/_8$
346	Power Minnow Suspending	12' 3"	5'–7'	Slow roll		Sus	P	Plastic	0.93	Nose	$^1/_2$	4	$4^1/_2$
347	Deep Baby N	12' 3"	6'–8'	Tight sway	Works well at 1.5 and 2 knots.		P	Plastic	0.70	Bib	$^5/_{16}$	2	$3^1/_8$
348	RMG Rellik Doc	12' 3"	8' 3"	Med. sway, tight roll	Australian favorite		P	Plastic	1.06	Bib	$^5/_8$	3	$3^7/_8$
349	Triho Min 180F	12' 3"		Medium roll		F	P	Plastic	0.93	Nose	$1^1/_2$	7	$7^1/_4$
350	Shad Rap Jointed JSR5	12' 3"	6'–8'	Fast sway, tight pitch	Great action.	Sus	P	Plastic	0.70	Bib	$^5/_{16}$	$2^3/_8$	$3^5/_8$
351	Stumpjumper 3 straight bib	12' 6"		Tight sway, shimmy		F	P	Plastic	0.79	Nose	$^3/_{16}$	$2^1/_4$	$2^3/_4$
352	Super Shad Rap 14	12' 6"	5'–9'	Tight sway, medium roll	Great action.		P	Plastic	1.08	Nose	$1^5/_8$	$5^1/_2$	$6^3/_4$

THE TEST RESULTS

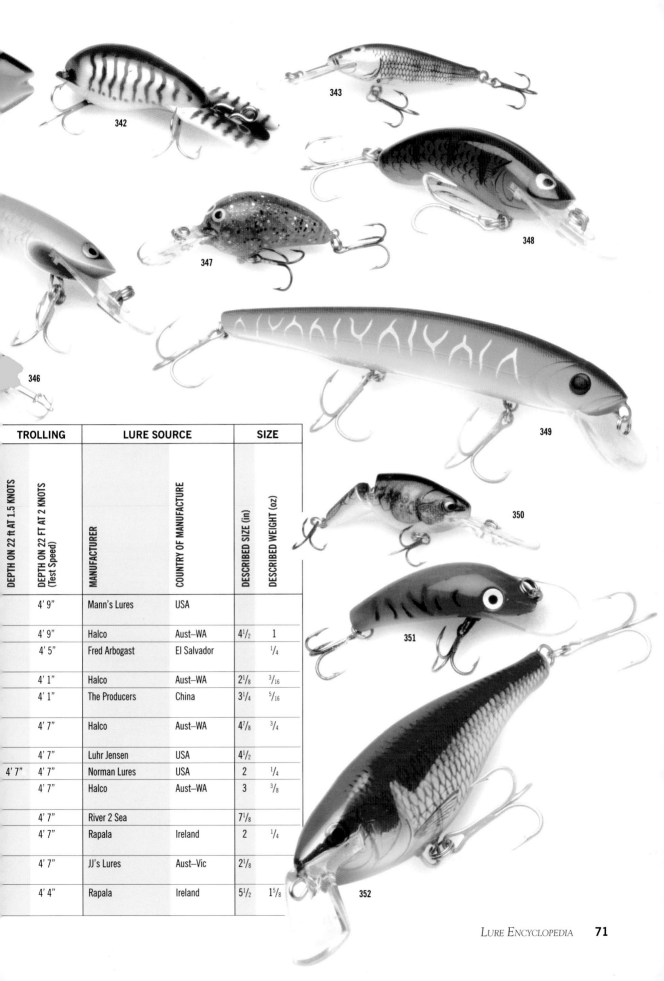

342
343
346
347
348
349
350
351
352

TROLLING		LURE SOURCE		SIZE	
DEPTH ON 22 ft AT 1.5 KNOTS	DEPTH ON 22 FT AT 2 KNOTS (Test Speed)	MANUFACTURER	COUNTRY OF MANUFACTURE	DESCRIBED SIZE (in)	DESCRIBED WEIGHT (oz)
	4' 9"	Mann's Lures	USA		
	4' 9"	Halco	Aust–WA	$4^1/_2$	1
	4' 5"	Fred Arbogast	El Salvador		$^1/_4$
	4' 1"	Halco	Aust–WA	$2^1/_8$	$^3/_{16}$
	4' 1"	The Producers	China	$3^1/_4$	$^5/_{16}$
	4' 7"	Halco	Aust–WA	$4^7/_8$	$^3/_4$
	4' 7"	Luhr Jensen	USA	$4^1/_2$	
4' 7"	4' 7"	Norman Lures	USA	2	$^1/_4$
	4' 7"	Halco	Aust–WA	3	$^3/_8$
	4' 7"	River 2 Sea		$7^1/_8$	
	4' 7"	Rapala	Ireland	2	$^1/_4$
	4' 7"	JJ's Lures	Aust–Vic	$2^1/_8$	
	4' 4"	Rapala	Ireland	$5^1/_2$	$1^5/_8$

NUMBER	LURE	DEPTH (FT) ON 66 FT	MAKER'S STATED DEPTH	ACTION	COMMENTS	FLOATING – SINKING – SUSPENDING	BODY MATERIAL PLASTIC – METAL – WOOD – RUBBER	BIB MATERIAL	WIDTH OF BIB (in)	TOW POINT	ACTUAL WEIGHT (oz)	ACTUAL BODY LENGTH (in)	LENGTH WITH BIB (in)
353	Barramundi Mauler	12' 6"		Med. sway			P	Plastic	0.89	Bib	$5/8$	$4^3/8$	$5^3/4$
354	Barramundi Mauler 6	12' 6"		Med. sway			P	Plastic	0.95	Bib	1	$5^1/4$	$6^3/4$
355	Rat-L-Trap Magnum Force	12' 6"		Tight sway	Large rattler. Good hardware	S	P	Bibless	0.51	Body	$1^1/8$	4	4
356	Willy's Worm No 1	12' 6"		Shimmy	Inexpensive but very successful		P	Plastic	0.64	Bib	$3/16$	$1^3/8$	$2^3/8$
357	Kwikfish K12	12' 6"		Wide sway	Works well at 2 knots.	F	P	Plastic	0.87	Body	$3/8$	$2^3/4$	$3^5/8$
358	Kwikfish K15	12' 6"		Wide sway		F	P	Plastic	1.10	Body	1	$3^5/8$	$5^1/4$
359	RMG Scorpion 90 STD	12' 9"	10'	Med. sway, tight roll	Rattle.		P	Plastic	1.08	Bib	$1/2$	$3^3/8$	$4^1/4$
360	Klawdad	12' 9"		Tight sway		F	P	Plastic	0.92	Bib	$3/8$	3	$3^3/4$
361	Rattlin' Fat Rap RFR-5	12' 9"		Med. sway, tight roll	Older style Rapala. Highly regarded	F	W	Plastic	0.72	Bib	$3/8$	2	$3^1/8$
362	Bandit 200 Series	12' 9"	4'–8'	Tight sway, tight roll	Great lure		P	Plastic	0.79	Bib	$5/16$	$2^1/8$	3
363	TD Hyper Crank	12' 9"		Med. sway	High quality lure		P	Metal	0.67	Bib	$1/4$	2	$2^7/8$
364	Invincible F15	12' 9"	10'	Wide roll		F	W	Plastic	0.93	Nose	1	6	$6^5/8$
365	Laser Pro 160 DD	13'	6' 6"	Slow tight sway	Rattle. Must have saltwater trolling lure		P	Plastic	0.83	Nose	$1^1/8$	$6^1/8$	7
366	Magnum Mag-18	13'		Slow med. sway		F	P	Plastic	0.89	Nose		7	$8^3/8$

353

354

356

357

358

TROLLING		LURE SOURCE		SIZE	
DEPTH ON 22 ft AT 1.5 KNOTS	DEPTH ON 22 FT AT 2 KNOTS (Test Speed)	MANUFACTURER	COUNTRY OF MANUFACTURE	DESCRIBED SIZE (in)	DESCRIBED WEIGHT (oz)
4' 7"		The Producers	China	$5^1/_2$	$^5/_8$
4' 7"		The Producers	China	$6^3/_4$	$^3/_4$
4' 9"		Bill Lewis Lures	USA		1
4' 4"		The Producers	China	$2^1/_4$	$^1/_8$
5' 1"		Luhr Jensen	USA	$3^5/_8$	$^3/_8$
5' 1"		Luhr Jensen	USA	$4^7/_8$	1
4' 9"		Halco	Aust—WA	$3^1/_2$	$^1/_2$
4' 9"		Luhr Jensen	Mexico		$^1/_2$
4' 9"		Rapala	Ireland	2	$^3/_8$
4' 9"		Bandit Lures	USA		
4' 9"		Team Diawa	Japan		
4' 9"		Nilsmaster	Finland	$5^7/_8$	1
4' 9"		Halco	Aust—WA	$6^1/_4$	1
4' 9"		Rapala	Ireland	$7^1/_8$	$1^3/_8$

361

362

363

364

355

LASER PRO

365

360

359

366

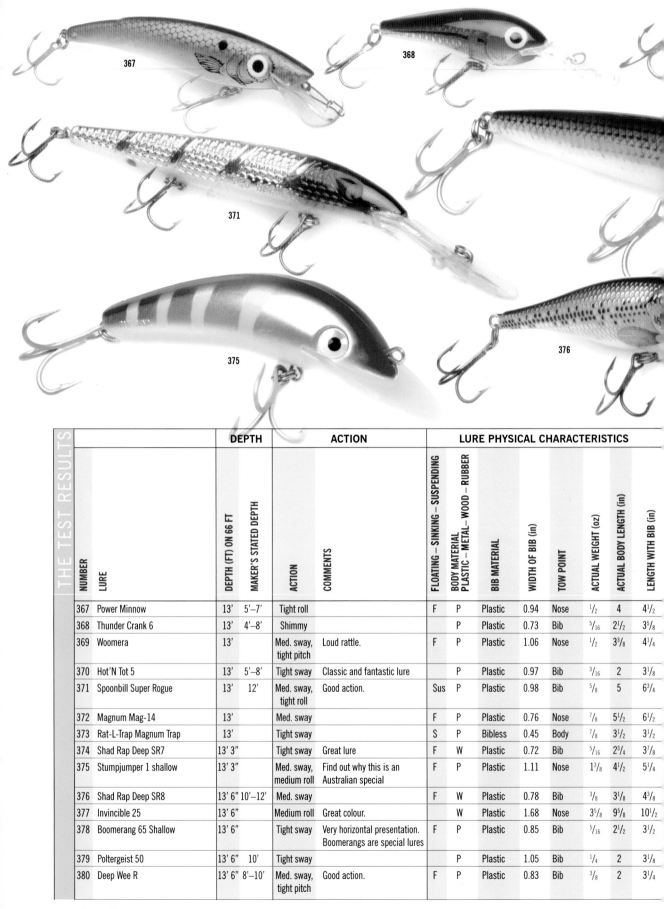

367

368

371

375

376

		DEPTH		ACTION		LURE PHYSICAL CHARACTERISTICS							
NUMBER	LURE	DEPTH (FT) ON 66 FT	MAKER'S STATED DEPTH	ACTION	COMMENTS	FLOATING – SINKING – SUSPENDING	BODY MATERIAL PLASTIC – METAL – WOOD – RUBBER	BIB MATERIAL	WIDTH OF BIB (in)	TOW POINT	ACTUAL WEIGHT (oz)	ACTUAL BODY LENGTH (in)	LENGTH WITH BIB (in)
367	Power Minnow	13'	5'–7'	Tight roll		F	P	Plastic	0.94	Nose	$^{1}/_{2}$	4	$4^{1}/_{2}$
368	Thunder Crank 6	13'	4'–8'	Shimmy			P	Plastic	0.73	Bib	$^{5}/_{16}$	$2^{1}/_{2}$	$3^{5}/_{8}$
369	Woomera	13'		Med. sway, tight pitch	Loud rattle.	F	P	Plastic	1.06	Nose	$^{1}/_{2}$	$3^{3}/_{8}$	$4^{1}/_{4}$
370	Hot'N Tot 5	13'	5'–8'	Tight sway	Classic and fantastic lure		P	Plastic	0.97	Bib	$^{3}/_{16}$	2	$3^{1}/_{8}$
371	Spoonbill Super Rogue	13'	12'	Med. sway, tight roll	Good action.	Sus	P	Plastic	0.98	Bib	$^{5}/_{8}$	5	$6^{3}/_{4}$
372	Magnum Mag-14	13'		Med. sway		F	P	Plastic	0.76	Nose	$^{7}/_{8}$	$5^{1}/_{2}$	$6^{1}/_{2}$
373	Rat-L-Trap Magnum Trap	13'		Tight sway		S	P	Bibless	0.45	Body	$^{7}/_{8}$	$3^{1}/_{2}$	$3^{1}/_{2}$
374	Shad Rap Deep SR7	13' 3"		Tight sway	Great lure	F	W	Plastic	0.72	Bib	$^{5}/_{16}$	$2^{3}/_{4}$	$3^{7}/_{8}$
375	Stumpjumper 1 shallow	13' 3"		Med. sway, medium roll	Find out why this is an Australian special	F	P	Plastic	1.11	Nose	$1^{3}/_{8}$	$4^{1}/_{2}$	$5^{1}/_{4}$
376	Shad Rap Deep SR8	13' 6"	10'–12'	Med. sway		F	W	Plastic	0.78	Bib	$^{3}/_{8}$	$3^{1}/_{8}$	$4^{3}/_{8}$
377	Invincible 25	13' 6"		Medium roll	Great colour.		W	Plastic	1.68	Nose	$3^{5}/_{8}$	$9^{5}/_{8}$	$10^{1}/_{2}$
378	Boomerang 65 Shallow	13' 6"		Tight sway	Very horizontal presentation. Boomerangs are special lures	F	P	Plastic	0.85	Bib	$^{5}/_{16}$	$2^{1}/_{2}$	$3^{1}/_{2}$
379	Poltergeist 50	13' 6"	10'	Tight sway			P	Plastic	1.05	Bib	$^{1}/_{4}$	2	$3^{1}/_{8}$
380	Deep Wee R	13' 6"	8'–10'	Med. sway, tight pitch	Good action.	F	P	Plastic	0.83	Bib	$^{3}/_{8}$	2	$3^{1}/_{4}$

TROLLING		LURE SOURCE		SIZE	
DEPTH ON 22 ft AT 1.5 KNOTS	DEPTH ON 22 FT AT 2 KNOTS (Test Speed)	MANUFACTURER	COUNTRY OF MANUFACTURE	DESCRIBED SIZE (in)	DESCRIBED WEIGHT (oz)
	4' 11"	Luhr Jensen	USA	$4^1/_2$	
	4' 5"	Storm	Estonia	$2^3/_8$	$^5/_{16}$
	4' 9"	Predatek	Aust–NSW		
	4' 11"	Storm	Estonia	2	$^3/_{16}$
	5'	Smithwick	USA	5	$^1/_2$
	5'	Rapala	Ireland	$5^1/_2$	$^3/_4$
	4' 5"	Bill Lewis Lures	USA		$^3/_4$
	4' 7"	Rapala	Ireland	$2^3/_4$	$^1/_4$
	4' 11"	JJ's Lures	Aust–Vic	$3^7/_8$	
	4' 9"	Rapala	Ireland	$3^1/_8$	$^3/_8$
	5' 5"	Nilsmaster	Finland	$9^7/_8$	$4^1/_4$
	4' 11"	Predatek	Aust–NSW	$2^1/_2$	
	5' 1"	Halco	Aust–WA	2	$^1/_4$
	5' 1"	Rebel	USA	2	$^3/_8$

NUMBER	LURE	DEPTH (FT) ON 66 FT	MAKER'S STATED DEPTH	ACTION	COMMENTS	FLOATING – SINKING – SUSPENDING	BODY MATERIAL PLASTIC – METAL – WOOD – RUBBER	BIB MATERIAL	WIDTH OF BIB (in)	TOW POINT	ACTUAL WEIGHT (oz)	ACTUAL BODY LENGTH (in)	LENGTH WITH BIB (in)
381	Wiggle Wart	13' 6"	6' 6"–12'	Med. sway	Great action. Exaggerated action at slower speed.		P	Plastic	0.85	Bib	$3/8$	2	3
382	Deep Crawfish	13' 6"	7'–9'	Tight sway	Great action.		P	Plastic	0.88	Bib	$5/16$	$2^{1}/_{4}$	$3^{1}/_{2}$
383	Rattlin' Fat Rap RFR-7	13' 6"		Med. sway	Now superceded but great lure	F	W	Plastic	0.78	Bib	$5/8$	$2^{7}/_{8}$	4
384	Bevy Shad 75	13' 6"		Tight sway, tight roll	Great action.	Sus	P	Plastic	0.68	Bib	$3/8$	3	4
385	RMG Scorpion 125 DD	13' 6"	13'	Tight sway			P	Plastic	1.22	Bib	$7/8$	$4^{7}/_{8}$	$6^{1}/_{8}$
386	Laser Pro 190 DD	13' 6"	6' 6"	Tight sway, tight roll	Better at 2.5 knots. Can even take marlin		P	Plastic	0.92	Nose	$1^{5}/_{8}$	7	$8^{1}/_{8}$
387	Stumpjumper 2 shallow	13' 9"		Med. sway, tight roll	Fantastic Australian lure	F	P	Plastic	0.83	Nose	$1/2$	$3^{1}/_{8}$	4
388	Fat Rap FR7	14'		Fast sway	My all time favorite lure	F	W	Plastic	0.79	Bib		$2^{7}/_{8}$	4
389	Willy's Worm No 2	14'		Med. sway	Good value and performance		P	Plastic	0.98	Bib	$5/16$	2	3
390	Willy's Worm No 3	14'		Med. sway			P	Plastic	0.87	Bib	$1/2$	$2^{1}/_{2}$	$3^{5}/_{8}$
391	Tilsan Barra	14'	11' 6"	Tight sway, tight roll	First rate lure	F	W	Plastic	0.80	Bib	$3/8$	$3^{1}/_{4}$	$4^{1}/_{2}$
392	Hot'N Tot 7	14'	7'–10'	Med. sway	Must have lure		P	Plastic	1.24	Bib	$3/8$	$2^{1}/_{2}$	$3^{3}/_{4}$
393	Bunyip	14'	12' 9"–14' 9"	Medium wide sway	Great action.		P	Plastic	1.02	Bib	$1/2$	$3^{3}/_{8}$	$4^{5}/_{8}$
394	Hydro Magnum	14'		Slow med. sway	Much better at 2.5 knots.	S	P	Plastic	0.71	Bib	$1^{1}/_{8}$	$4^{3}/_{4}$	$6^{1}/_{4}$

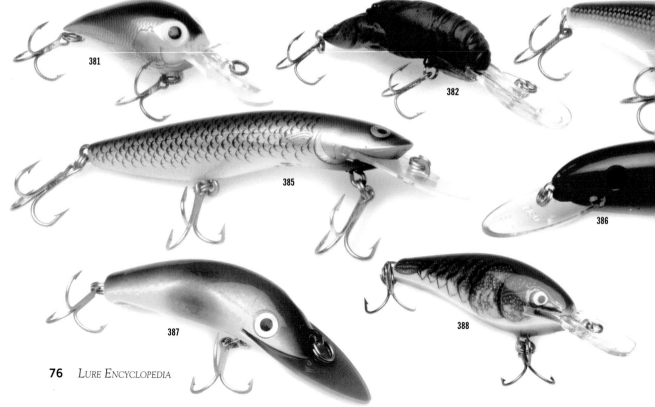

381

382

385

386

387

388

TROLLING		LURE SOURCE		SIZE	
DEPTH ON 22 ft AT 1.5 KNOTS	DEPTH ON 22 FT AT 2 KNOTS (Test Speed)	MANUFACTURER	COUNTRY OF MANUFACTURE	DESCRIBED SIZE (in)	DESCRIBED WEIGHT (oz)
5' 1"	5' 1"	Storm	Estonia	2	$3/8$
	5' 1"	Rebel	Mexico	$2^1/4$	$1/4$
	5' 1"	Rapala	Ireland	$2^3/4$	$5/8$
	4' 7"	Lucky Craft Lures	Japan	3	$3/8$
	5' 1"	Halco	Aust–WA	$4^7/8$	$3/4$
	5' 1"	Halco	Aust–WA	$7^1/4$	$1^5/8$
	5' 1"	JJ's Lures	Aust–Vic	3	
	5' 1"	Rapala	Ireland	$2^3/4$	$1/2$
	5' 2"	The Producers	China		$1/4$
	5' 2"	The Producers	China	$3^1/2$	$1/2$
	4' 9"	Halco	Aust–WA	$3^1/8$	$5/8$
	5' 2"	Storm	Estonia	$2^3/4$	$3/8$
	5' 2"	Predatek	Aust–NSW		$5/8$
	4' 9"	Yo-Zuri Lures	Japan	$4^3/4$	$5/8$

390

391

392

384

383

393

389

394

395   **396**

399   **400**

NUMBER	LURE	DEPTH (FT) ON 66 FT	MAKER'S STATED DEPTH	ACTION	COMMENTS	FLOATING – SINKING – SUSPENDING	BODY MATERIAL PLASTIC – METAL – WOOD – RUBBER	BIB MATERIAL	WIDTH OF BIB (in)	TOW POINT	ACTUAL WEIGHT (oz)	ACTUAL BODY LENGTH (in)	LENGTH WITH BIB (in)
		DEPTH		**ACTION**		**LURE PHYSICAL CHARACTERISTICS**							
395	Midive Min 140S	14'		Slow tight sway, tight roll		S	P	Plastic	0.85	Bib	1 3/4	5³/₈	7¹/₈
396	Hellbender Baby	14' 3"		Med. sway, tight roll	Classic special lure	F	P	Metal	0.87	Bib	¹/₄	2¹/₈	3¹/₈
397	Mud Bug 5/8oz	14' 3"		Medium roll	Great action and performance.	F	P	Metal	1.04	Bib	¹/₂	2¹/₂	3¹/₂
398	Frenzy Diving Minnow	14' 3" 10'		Medium roll		F	P	Plastic	0.90	Bib	¹/₂	4	5¹/₄
399	RMG Scorpion 150 STD	14' 6" 11' 6"		Medium roll		F	P	Plastic	1.08	Nose	1¹/₈	5⁷/₈	6³/₄
400	Hydro Squirt	14' 6"		Med. wobble, tight roll	Excellent action. Skirt looks great. One of top lures.	F	P	Plastic	0.92	Bib	1¹/₂	3⁷/₈	5⁵/₈
401	Stumpjumper 2 round bib	14' 6"		Med. sway, tight roll	Good action.	F	P	Plastic	0.93	Nose	¹/₂	3¹/₈	3⁷/₈
402	Kill'r B-II	14' 6" 0–13' 9"		Med. sway, tight pitch	Great deep diving Bagley	F	W	Plastic	1.13	Bib	¹/₂	2³/₈	3⁷/₈
403	Bandit 400 Series	14' 6" 12'–15'		Med. sway, med. pitch	Great action. Lateral movement.		P	Plastic	1.11	Bib	⁵/₈	2⁷/₈	4³/₈
404	Boomerang 65 Medium	14' 6"		Med. sway		F	P	Plastic	0.93	Bib	⁵/₁₆	2⁵/₈	3⁵/₈
405	Hot Lips Express 1/4oz	14' 6" 12'–15'		Med. sway	Great action.		P	Plastic	1.19	Bib	³/₈	2¹/₈	3¹/₂
406	Combat	14' 9" 8' 3"–1		Med. sway	Great action and lateral movement at slower speed	F	P	Plastic	0.79	Bib	¹/₄	2	2⁷/₈
407	Hardcore SH-60SP	14' 9"		Tight sway	Top finish and quality lure	Sus	P	Plastic	0.65	Bib	³/₁₆	2³/₈	3⁵/₈
408	Lightning Minnow #2	14' 9"		Shimmy			P	Plastic	0.66	Bib	¹/₄	2³/₈	3⁵/₈

THE TEST RESULTS

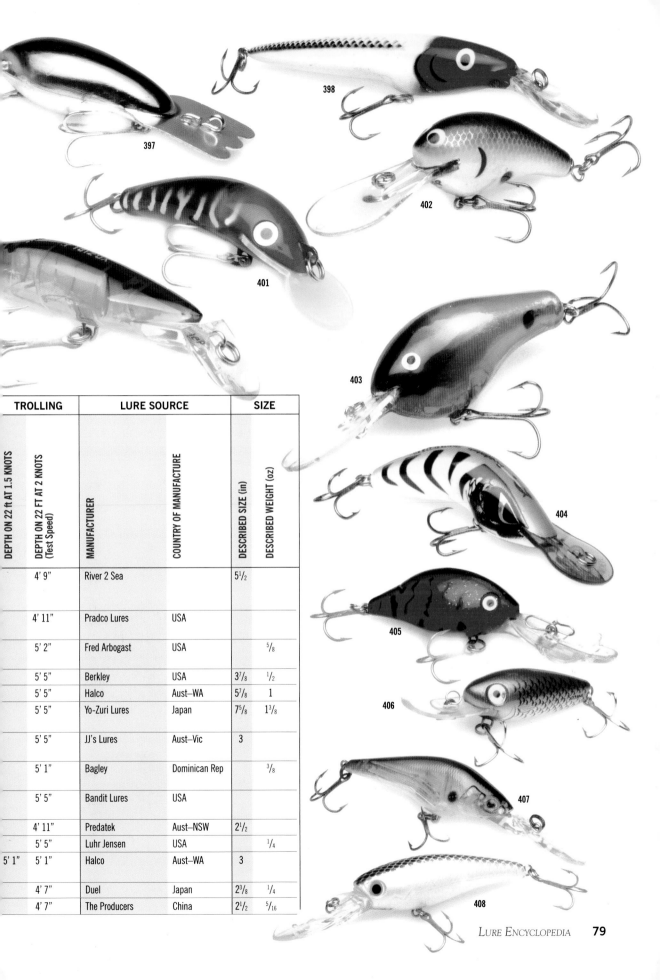

397

398

401

402

403

404

405

406

407

408

TROLLING		LURE SOURCE		SIZE	
DEPTH ON 22 ft AT 1.5 KNOTS	DEPTH ON 22 FT AT 2 KNOTS (Test Speed)	MANUFACTURER	COUNTRY OF MANUFACTURE	DESCRIBED SIZE (in)	DESCRIBED WEIGHT (oz)
	4' 9"	River 2 Sea		5$\frac{1}{2}$	
	4' 11"	Pradco Lures	USA		
	5' 2"	Fred Arbogast	USA		$\frac{5}{8}$
	5' 5"	Berkley	USA	3$\frac{7}{8}$	$\frac{1}{2}$
	5' 5"	Halco	Aust—WA	5$\frac{7}{8}$	1
	5' 5"	Yo-Zuri Lures	Japan	7$\frac{5}{8}$	1$\frac{3}{8}$
	5' 5"	JJ's Lures	Aust—Vic	3	
	5' 1"	Bagley	Dominican Rep		$\frac{3}{8}$
	5' 5"	Bandit Lures	USA		
	4' 11"	Predatek	Aust—NSW	2$\frac{1}{2}$	
	5' 5"	Luhr Jensen	USA		$\frac{1}{4}$
5' 1"	5' 1"	Halco	Aust—WA	3	
	4' 7"	Duel	Japan	2$\frac{3}{8}$	$\frac{1}{4}$
	4' 7"	The Producers	China	2$\frac{1}{2}$	$\frac{5}{16}$

THE TEST RESULTS

NUMBER	LURE	DEPTH: DEPTH (FT) ON 66 FT	DEPTH: MAKER'S STATED DEPTH	ACTION: ACTION	ACTION: COMMENTS	LURE PHYSICAL CHARACTERISTICS: FLOATING – SINKING – SUSPENDING	BODY MATERIAL PLASTIC – METAL – WOOD – RUBBER	BIB MATERIAL	WIDTH OF BIB (in)	TOW POINT	ACTUAL WEIGHT (oz)	ACTUAL BODY LENGTH (in)	LENGTH WITH BIB (in)
409	Magnum CD-11	14' 9"		Med. sway	Great action at 2.5 knots.	S	P	Metal	0.76	Bib	1	4 1/4	5 3/4
410	10+	15'	10'	Tight sway, tight roll	One of the best lures made		P	Plastic	0.96	Bib	5/16	1 7/8	3 1/8
411	Pro's Choice Lil Lonni	15'	12'	Tight sway	Quality crankbait		P	Plastic	0.97	Bib	1/2	2 3/8	4 1/8
412	Shad Rap Suspending RS5	15'		Tight sway	A truly great suspending lure	Sus	P	Plastic	0.74	Bib	5/16	2 1/2	3 1/2
413	Deep Flat A	15'		Tight sway, tight roll	Versatile with unusual features	P	Plastic		0.83	Bib	3/8	2 1/2	3 5/8
414	Model 6A	15'		Tight sway	One of my favorite lures		P	Plastic	0.82	Bib	3/8	2 1/8	3 1/4
415	Stumpjumper 2 deep bib	15'		Med. sway, tight roll	Good action. More exaggerated at slower speed.	F	P	Plastic	0.97	Nose	1/2	3 1/8	4
416	Invincible DR 12 cm	15'		Med. sway, med. pitch	Great action.	S	W	Plastic	0.94	Nose	3/4	4 1/2	5 7/8
417	Hot'N Tot (USA made)	15' 3"		Med. wide sway	Excellent action. Lateral m movement. Better at 1.5 knots.	F	P	Plastic	1.10	Body	3/8	2 3/8	3 3/4
418	Magnum wiggle wart (US made)	15' 3"		Med. sway, tight pitch	Excellent action both speeds. Loud rattle. Trailing hook stable.	F	P	Plastic	1.01	Bib	3/4	2 1/2	3 3/4
419	Hellbender Midget	15' 6"		Med. sway, tight pitch	Good action. Lateral movemement.	F	P	Metal	0.97	Bib	3/8	2 5/8	3 3/4
420	RMG Scorpion 90 DD	15' 6"	13'	Tight roll	Good depth, tight action for bib size.	F	P	Plastic	1.36	Bib	1/2	3 3/8	4 1/2
421	Deep Wart	15' 6"		Med. sway	Great action. Some lateral movement.		P	Plastic	0.92	Bib	3/8	2	3 1/4
422	Avoidance Behaviour Lure	15' 6"		Tight sway, med. pitch	Good erratic action caused by blade.	F	P	Plastic	1.13	Bib	5/8	2 7/8	4 3/8

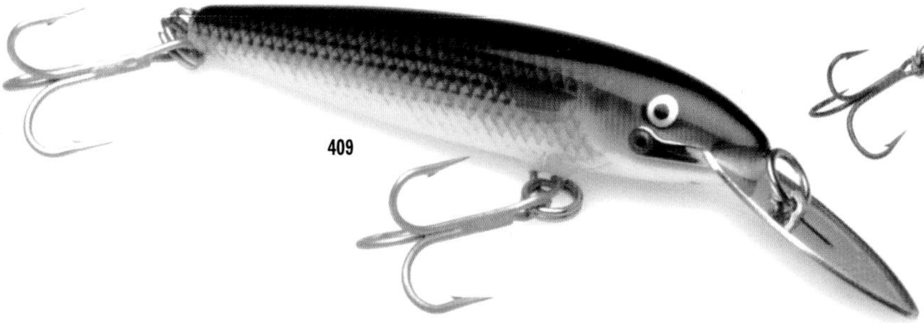
409

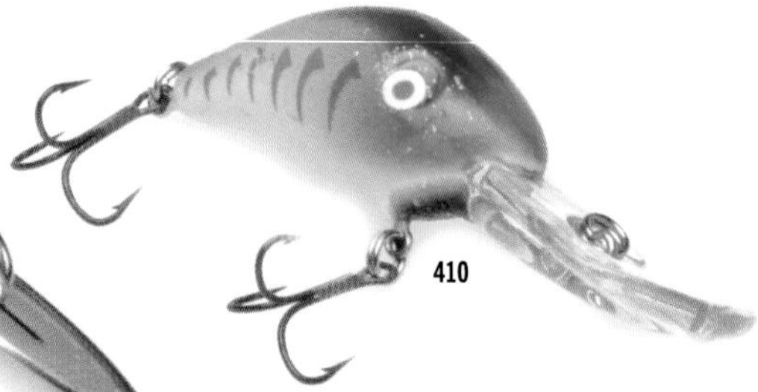
410

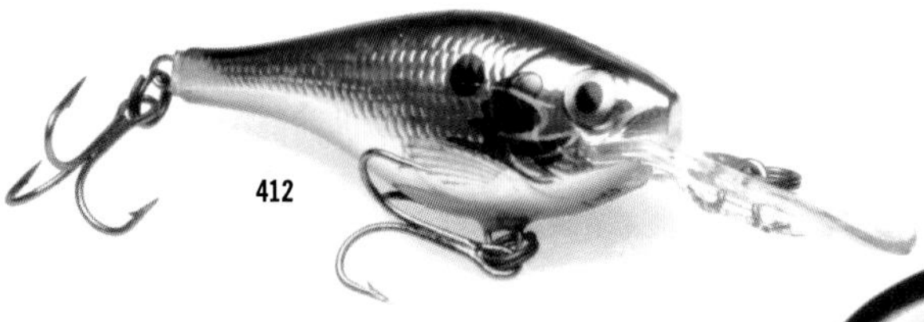
412

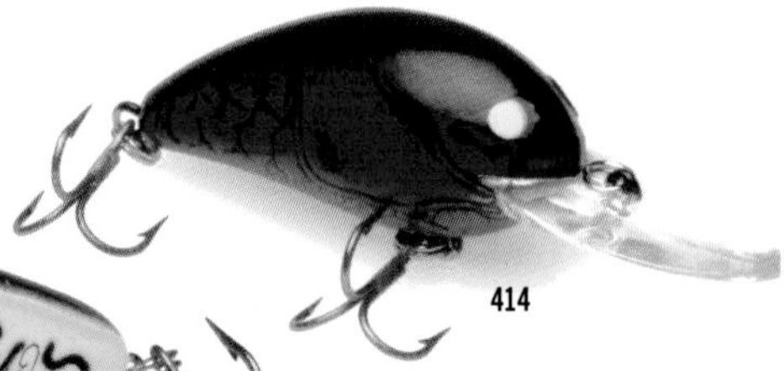
414

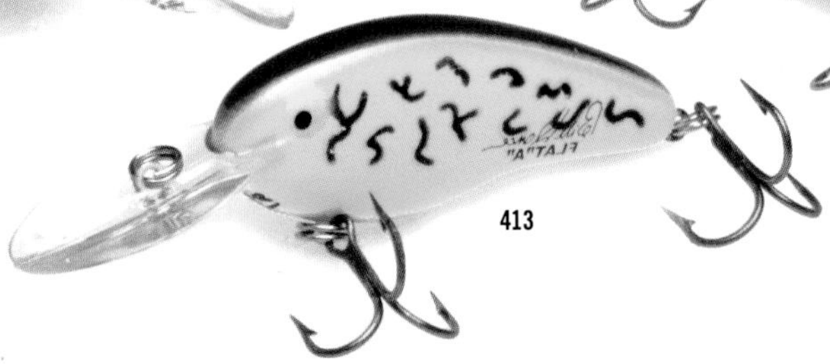

413

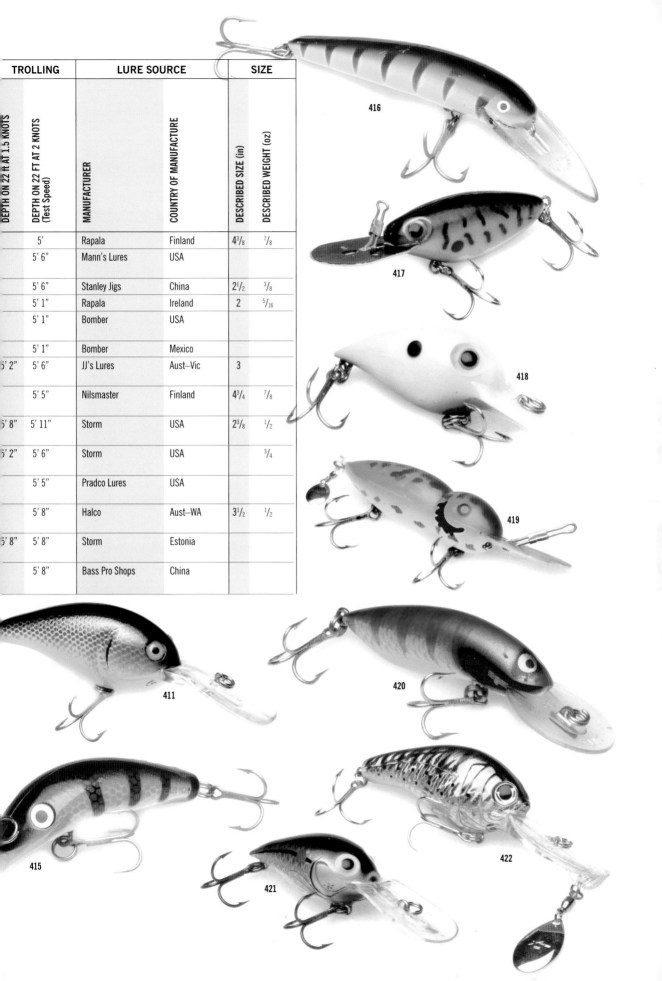

TROLLING		LURE SOURCE		SIZE	
DEPTH ON 22 ft AT 1.5 KNOTS	DEPTH ON 22 FT AT 2 KNOTS (Test Speed)	MANUFACTURER	COUNTRY OF MANUFACTURE	DESCRIBED SIZE (in)	DESCRIBED WEIGHT (oz)
	5'	Rapala	Finland	$4^3/_8$	$^7/_8$
	5' 6"	Mann's Lures	USA		
	5' 6"	Stanley Jigs	China	$2^1/_2$	$^3/_8$
	5' 1"	Rapala	Ireland	2	$^5/_{16}$
	5' 1"	Bomber	USA		
	5' 1"	Bomber	Mexico		
5' 2"	5' 6"	JJ's Lures	Aust—Vic	3	
	5' 5"	Nilsmaster	Finland	$4^3/_4$	$^7/_8$
5' 8"	5' 11"	Storm	USA	$2^3/_8$	$^1/_2$
5' 2"	5' 6"	Storm	USA		$^3/_4$
	5' 5"	Pradco Lures	USA		
	5' 8"	Halco	Aust—WA	$3^1/_2$	$^1/_2$
5' 8"	5' 8"	Storm	Estonia		
	5' 8"	Bass Pro Shops	China		

416

417

418

419

411

420

415

421

422

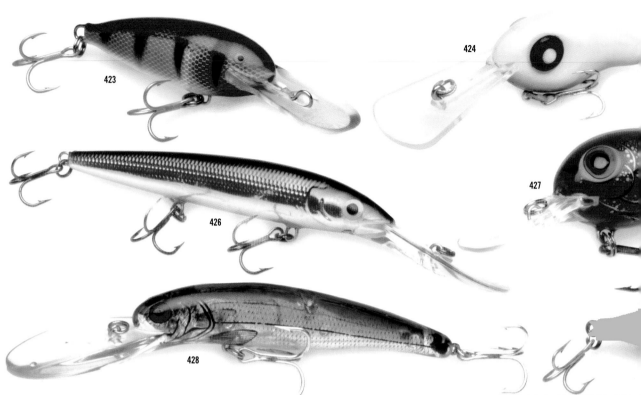

		DEPTH		ACTION		LURE PHYSICAL CHARACTERISTICS							
NUMBER	LURE	DEPTH (FT) ON 66 FT	MAKER'S STATED DEPTH	ACTION	COMMENTS	FLOATING – SINKING – SUSPENDING	BODY MATERIAL PLASTIC – METAL– WOOD – RUBBER	BIB MATERIAL	WIDTH OF BIB (in)	TOW POINT	ACTUAL WEIGHT (oz)	ACTUAL BODY LENGTH (in)	LENGTH WITH BIB (in)
423	Haka Down Deep	15' 6"		Tight sway	Looks good both speeds.		W	Plastic	0.89	Bib	$5/16$	$2^5/8$	$3^3/4$
424	Probe	15' 6"		Med. sway, tight pitch	Great action.	F	P	Plastic	1.20	Bib	$3/8$	2	$3^3/8$
425	Frenzy	15' 6"	10'	Med. sway	Quality lure	F	P	Plastic	0.89	Bib	$1/2$	$2^3/4$	$4^1/8$
426	Husky Jerk Deep DHJ-12	15' 6"		Med. sway,	Good depth	Sus	P	Plastic	0.87	Bib	$1/2$	$4^5/8$	$6^3/8$
427	Wiggle Wart	15' 9"	12'–17'	Med. sway	Great action at both speeds.		P	Plastic	1.03	Bib	$3/4$	$2^1/2$	$3^3/4$
428	Long A Minnow	15' 9"		Med. sway	Extremely popular minnow		P	Plastic	1.02	Bib	$3/4$	$4^1/2$	$6^1/8$
429	Tilsan Bass	16'	14' 9"	Tight sway, tight pitch	Nice diving and action	S	W	Plastic	0.93	Bib	$1/4$	$2^1/4$	$3^1/2$
430	Wiggle 'O'	16'	13' 9"– 17' 9"	Med. wide sway	Better slower. Great colour.		P	Plastic	0.85	Bib	$3/8$	2	3
431	Viper 150	16'		Tight sway, tight roll	Excellent action at 2.5 knots.		P	Plastic	1.07	Nose	1	$5^1/2$	$6^1/2$
432	Boomerang 80M	16'		Tight sway, tight roll	A must have Australian lure		P	Plastic	1.05	Bib	$5/8$	$3^1/4$	$4^3/8$
433	Stretch 10+	16'	10'	Med. sway	Works well both speeds.		P	Plastic	0.96	Bib	$1/2$	$3^1/4$	$4^1/2$
434	Premier Pro-Model Seri	16'	10'–12'	Med. sway	Quality crankbait		P	Plastic	1.10	Bib	$5/8$	$2^5/8$	$4^1/2$
435	Model 7A	16'		Tight sway, tight pitch			P	Plastic	0.86	Bib	$1/2$	$2^5/8$	$3^3/4$
436	Deep Z	16'		Tight sway, tight pitch	Great colour.	F	P	Plastic	0.96	Bib	$1/2$	$2^3/4$	$4^1/8$

THE TEST RESULTS

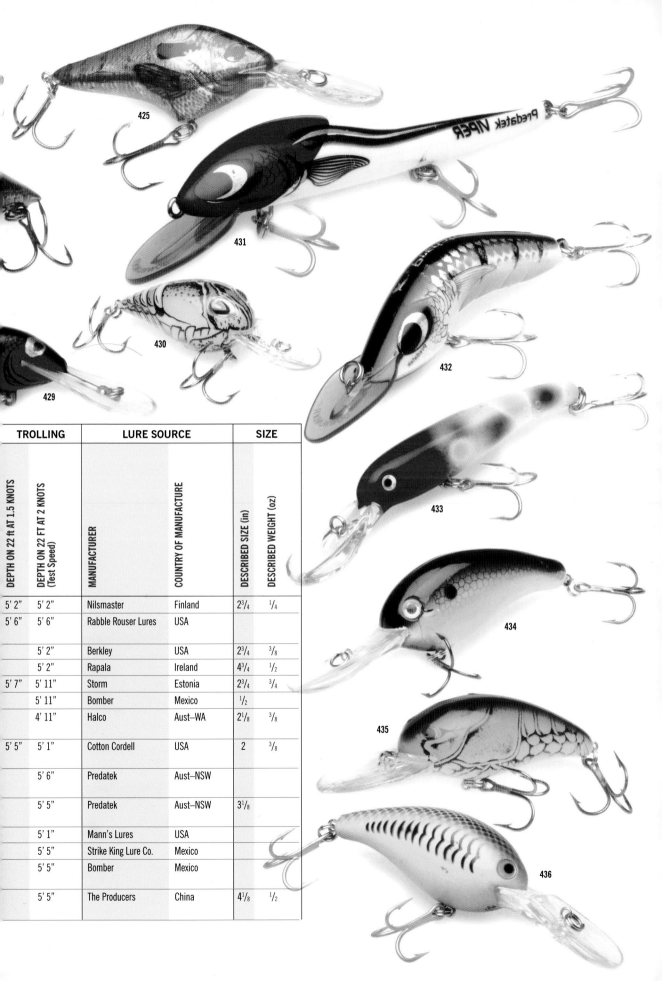

TROLLING		LURE SOURCE		SIZE	
DEPTH ON 22 ft AT 1.5 KNOTS	DEPTH ON 22 FT AT 2 KNOTS (Test Speed)	MANUFACTURER	COUNTRY OF MANUFACTURE	DESCRIBED SIZE (in)	DESCRIBED WEIGHT (oz)
5' 2"	5' 2"	Nilsmaster	Finland	$2^3/_4$	$^1/_4$
5' 6"	5' 6"	Rabble Rouser Lures	USA		
	5' 2"	Berkley	USA	$2^3/_4$	$^3/_8$
	5' 2"	Rapala	Ireland	$4^3/_4$	$^1/_2$
5' 7"	5' 11"	Storm	Estonia	$2^3/_4$	$^3/_4$
	5' 11"	Bomber	Mexico	$^1/_2$	
	4' 11"	Halco	Aust—WA	$2^1/_8$	$^3/_8$
5' 5"	5' 1"	Cotton Cordell	USA	2	$^3/_8$
	5' 6"	Predatek	Aust—NSW		
	5' 5"	Predatek	Aust—NSW	$3^1/_8$	
	5' 1"	Mann's Lures	USA		
	5' 5"	Strike King Lure Co.	Mexico		
	5' 5"	Bomber	Mexico		
	5' 5"	The Producers	China	$4^1/_8$	$^1/_2$

NUMBER	LURE	DEPTH (FT) ON 66 FT	MAKER'S STATED DEPTH	ACTION	COMMENTS	FLOATING – SINKING – SUSPENDING	BODY MATERIAL PLASTIC – METAL – WOOD – RUBBER	BIB MATERIAL	WIDTH OF BIB (in)	TOW POINT	ACTUAL WEIGHT (oz)	ACTUAL BODY LENGTH (in)	LENGTH WITH BIB (in)
437	Invincible DR15	16'	13'	Medium roll			W	Metal	0.87	Nose	$1\frac{1}{8}$	6	$7\frac{1}{8}$
438	Deep ThunderStick	16'	10'–14'	Med. sway, tight roll	Great finish	S	P	Bibless	0.88	Bib	$\frac{5}{8}$	$4\frac{1}{2}$	6
439	Hydro Magnum 140 mm	16'		Med. sway, medium roll	Great saltwater lure	S	P	Plastic	0.81	Bib	$1\frac{3}{4}$	$5\frac{1}{2}$	$7\frac{3}{8}$
440	Boomerang 65	16' 3"		Fast sway	Colors look great.	F	P	Plastic	1.06	Bib	$\frac{3}{8}$	$2\frac{5}{8}$	$3\frac{7}{8}$
441	Boomerang 65	16' 3"		Tight sway, med. pitch	Great kicking action both speeds.	F	P	Plastic	1.27	Bib	$\frac{3}{8}$	$2\frac{5}{8}$	$4\frac{1}{8}$
442	Sliver Jointed 20	16' 3"		Tight sway, medium roll	Much better at speed		P	Metal	0.74	Bib		8	$9\frac{3}{8}$
443	Magnum CD-9	16' 6"		Tight sway	Excellent action at 2.5 knots.	S	W	Metal	0.76	Bib	$\frac{5}{8}$	$3\frac{5}{8}$	5
444	Scale Raza 20+	16' 6"	19' 6"	Med. sway, tight pitch	Great action. Unique erratic movement. Best lure of tests.		P	Plastic	1.38	Bib	$\frac{5}{8}$	$4\frac{5}{8}$	$6\frac{1}{4}$
445	Spoonbill	16' 6"		Med. sway, medium roll	Great action.		P	Plastic	0.94	Bib	$\frac{1}{2}$	$3\frac{1}{4}$	$4\frac{1}{2}$
446	Shad Rap Suspending RS7	16' 6"		Tight sway		Sus	W	Plastic	0.85	Bib	$\frac{1}{2}$	3	$4\frac{3}{8}$
447	Moonsault CB-350	16' 6"		Med. sway	Championship lure. Best quality	F	P	Plastic	0.81	Bib	$\frac{1}{2}$	$2\frac{1}{2}$	$3\frac{7}{8}$
448	Risto Rap RR-8	16' 6"		Med. sway, tight roll	Good lure already out of production	F	W	Plastic	0.93	Bib		3	$4\frac{7}{8}$
449	Shad Rap Deep SR9	16' 9"	12'–14'	Med. sway, tight roll	Great barramundi lure	F	W	Plastic	0.91	Bib	$\frac{1}{2}$	$3\frac{5}{8}$	$5\frac{1}{8}$
450	RMG Poltergeist 80	16' 9"	16' 6"	Med. sway	Strong following in Australia	S	P	Plastic	1.42	Bib	$\frac{5}{8}$	$3\frac{1}{8}$	$4\frac{3}{4}$

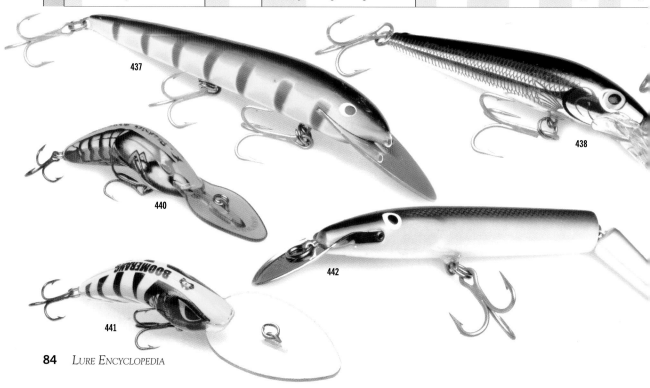

437

438

440

442

441

TROLLING		LURE SOURCE		SIZE	
DEPTH ON 22 ft AT 1.5 KNOTS	DEPTH ON 22 FT AT 2 KNOTS (Test Speed)	MANUFACTURER	COUNTRY OF MANUFACTURE	DESCRIBED SIZE (in)	DESCRIBED WEIGHT (oz)
	5' 5"	Nilsmaster	Finland	$5\frac{7}{8}$	1
	5' 5"	Storm	Estonia		
	5' 5"	Yo-Zuri Lures	Japan	$5\frac{1}{2}$	$1\frac{7}{8}$
	5' 6"	Predatek	Aust–NSW	$2\frac{1}{2}$	
6' 1"	6'	Predatek	Aust–NSW	$2\frac{1}{2}$	
	5' 2"	Rapala	Ireland	$7\frac{7}{8}$	$1\frac{3}{8}$
	5' 5"	Rapala	Ireland	$3\frac{1}{2}$	$\frac{5}{8}$
6' 2"	5' 11"	DK Lures	Aust–Qld		
	5' 6"	Predatek	Aust–NSW		
	5' 6"	Rapala	Ireland	$2\frac{3}{4}$	$\frac{3}{8}$
	5' 6"	Lucky Craft Lures	Japan		$\frac{1}{2}$
	5' 6"	Rapala	Ireland	$3\frac{1}{8}$	$\frac{3}{4}$
	5' 2"	Rapala	Ireland	$3\frac{4}{8}$	$\frac{1}{2}$
	6' 2"	Halco	Aust–WA	$3\frac{1}{8}$	$\frac{5}{8}$

445

446

447

448

449

439

443

444

450

		DEPTH		ACTION		LURE PHYSICAL CHARACTERISTICS							
NUMBER	LURE	DEPTH (FT) ON 66 FT	MAKER'S STATED DEPTH	ACTION	COMMENTS	FLOATING – SINKING – SUSPENDING	BODY MATERIAL PLASTIC – METAL – WOOD – RUBBER	BIB MATERIAL	WIDTH OF BIB (in)	TOW POINT	ACTUAL WEIGHT (oz)	ACTUAL BODY LENGTH (in)	LENGTH WITH BIB (in)
451	Suspending Fat Free Fry	17'		Tight sway	Very popular crankbait	Sus	P	Plastic	0.86	Bib	$^3/_8$	2	$3^1/_4$
452	Fat Free Fry	17'		Tight sway			P	Plastic	0.87	Bib	$^5/_{16}$	2	$3^1/_4$
453	Giant Trembler	17'	6' 6"	Tight sway	Works at high speeds for pelagic fish	S	P	Bibless		Body	$4^1/_2$	7	7
454	Double Downer #3	17'		Med. sway	Great action. Lateral movement.		P	Metal	1.10	Bib	$^1/_2$	$2^1/_2$	$3^7/_8$
455	Power Dive Minnow 1/2 oz	17'	19' 6"	Fast tight sway	Popular and successful bait		P	Plastic	1.15	Bib	$^5/_{16}$	$3^1/_4$	$4^5/_8$
456	Rattlin' Rogue ASSRB1200	17' 3"	10'	Med. sway	Rattles for extra attraction	Sus	P	Plastic	0.92	Bib	$^1/_2$	$4^1/_2$	$6^1/_8$
457	Thunder Crank	17' 3"	8'–15'	Med. sway	Durable and successful		P	Plastic	0.87	Bib	$^3/_8$	3	$4^3/_8$
458	Deep Husky Jerk DHJ-101	7' 3"		Med. sway		Sus		Plastic	0.75	Bib	$^3/_8$	$3^3/_4$	$5^1/_4$
459	15+	17' 6"	15'	Med. sway	Many applications for this classic	F	P	Plastic	1.22	Bib	$^1/_2$	$2^1/_4$	$3^3/_4$
460	Jumbo DD	17' 6"		Med. sway, med. pitch	Great erratic action. Better at 2.5 knots. A real winner.	F	W	Plastic	1.40	Nose		$4^1/_2$	$5^1/_2$
461	Crank'n Shad	17' 6"	8'	Tight sway	Another quality Yo-Zuri	F	P	Plastic	0.85	Bib	$^3/_8$	$2^7/_8$	$4^3/_8$
462	Down Deep Husky Jerk 12	17' 6"		Med. wide sway, tight pitch		Sus	P	Plastic	0.87	Bib	$^5/_8$	$4^5/_8$	$6^1/_4$
463	Wally Minnow CS8	17' 9"	20' 6"	Med. wide sway	Good action.	Sus	P	Plastic	1.08	Bib	$^1/_2$	4	$5^1/_2$
464	RMG Scorpion 150 DD	17' 9"	16' 6"	Tight sway, tight roll	Unique bib design taking the world by storm		P	Plastic	1.35	Bib	$1^1/_8$	$5^7/_8$	$7^1/_8$

TROLLING		LURE SOURCE		SIZE	
DEPTH ON 22 ft AT 1.5 KNOTS	DEPTH ON 22 FT AT 2 KNOTS (Test Speed)	MANUFACTURER	COUNTRY OF MANUFACTURE	DESCRIBED SIZE (in)	DESCRIBED WEIGHT (oz)
	5' 2"	Excalibur	USA		$^3/_8$
	5' 2"	Excalibur	USA		
	6' 2"	Halco	Aust—WA	7	$4^3/_8$
	5' 8"	The Producers	China	$3^3/_4$	$^1/_2$
	5' 8"	Luhr Jensen	USA	$4^3/_4$	$^1/_2$
	5' 5"	Smithwick	Mexico	6	$^3/_8$
	5' 5"	Storm	Estonia	$3^1/_8$	$^3/_8$
	5' 5"	Rapala	Ireland	$3^7/_8$	$^3/_8$
	5' 8"	Mann's Lures	USA		
5' 11"		Nilsmaster	Finland		
	5' 5"	Yo-Zuri Lures	Japan	$2^7/_8$	
	5' 5"	Rapala	Ireland	$4^3/_4$	$^1/_2$
	5' 6"	Cotton Cordell	USA	$4^1/_2$	$^1/_2$
5' 11"		Halco	Aust—WA	$5^7/_8$	1

NUMBER	LURE	DEPTH (FT) ON 66 FT	MAKER'S STATED DEPTH	ACTION	COMMENTS	FLOATING – SINKING – SUSPENDING	BODY MATERIAL PLASTIC – METAL – WOOD – RUBBER	BIB MATERIAL	WIDTH OF BIB (in)	TOW POINT	ACTUAL WEIGHT (oz)	ACTUAL BODY LENGTH (in)	LENGTH WITH BIB (in)
465	Mud Bug	18'		Med. wide sway	Big and extremely successful	F	P	Metal	1.25	Bib		3	$4^1/_4$
466	Magnum CD-14	18'		Med. sway, tight roll	Better at 2.5 knots. Number one saltwater trolling lure	S	P	Metal	0.83	Bib	$1^3/_8$	$5^1/_4$	$6^7/_8$
467	Cisco Kid 1800	18' 3"		Wide sway, tight roll	Old favorite		P	Metal	1.64	Bib	$3^3/_8$	$7^5/_8$	$9^1/_4$
468	Heavy Duty Stretch 12+	18' 3"		Tight sway	Great action and sound. Better at 3 knots or above		P	Plastic	1.26	Bib	$1^5/_8$	$5^7/_8$	$7^7/_8$
469	Suspend DD-22	18' 6"	15'–18'	Med. sway	Deep diver for special places	Sus	P	Plastic	1.19	Bib	1	3	$5^1/_8$
470	Power Dive Minnow	18' 6"	29' 6"	Med. sway, tight roll	Strong lateral movement.		P	Plastic	1.51	Bib		4	$5^7/_8$
471	Hellbender - Magnum	18' 6"		Med. wide sway	Excellent action. Lateral movement. One of best lures.	F	P	Metal	1.35	Bib		$3^1/_2$	$5^1/_4$
472	Prime DD Crankbait 25	18' 9"	10'–15'	Med. sway, tight roll	Excellent action—steep dive. Rattle.	P	P		0.95	Bib	$1/_2$	$2^1/_2$	$4^1/_8$
473	Boof Bait	19'	12'	Med. sway	Top barramundi lure in Australia	P	P		1.19	Bib	$3/_4$	$4^5/_8$	$6^1/_8$
474	DD-22	19'	15'–18'	Med. sway			P	Plastic	1.22	Bib	1	3	$5^1/_8$
475	Long A	19'		Med. sway			P	Plastic	0.94	Bib	$3/_8$	$3^1/_2$	$4^3/_4$
476	Boomerang 80	19' 3"		Med. sway	Much better at 1.5 knots.	F	P	Plastic	1.41	Bib	$3/_4$	$3^1/_4$	5
477	Suspending Fat Free Shad	19' 6"		Med. sway	Deep diver suspending bonus	Sus	P	Plastic	1.10	Bib	$5/_8$	$2^1/_2$	4
478	Stretch 20+	19' 9"	20'	Med. sway	Better at 2 knots.		P	Plastic	1.40	Bib	$7/_8$	$4^1/_2$	$6^3/_8$

465

466

467

468

TROLLING		LURE SOURCE		SIZE	
DEPTH ON 22 ft AT 1.5 KNOTS	DEPTH ON 22 FT AT 2 KNOTS (Test Speed)	MANUFACTURER	COUNTRY OF MANUFACTURE	DESCRIBED SIZE (in)	DESCRIBED WEIGHT (oz)
	6' 8"	Fred Arbogast	USA		
	5' 7"	Rapala	Ireland	$5^1/_2$	$1^1/_4$
	6'	Suick Lures	USA	$9^1/_2$	$3^5/_8$
	5' 7"	Mann's Lures	USA		$1^1/_4$
	6' 2"	Norman Lures	USA	3	$^5/_8$
	6' 2"	Luhr Jensen	USA	6	$^3/_4$
	6' 2"	Pradco Lures	USA		
	5' 8"	Spro	China		
	5' 11"	Mann's Lures	USA		$^1/_2$
	6' 2"	Norman Lures	USA	3	$^5/_8$
	5' 11"	Bomber	Mexico		$^3/_8$
6' 2"	6' 1"	Predatek	Aust–NSW	$3^1/_8$	
	6'	Excalibur	USA		
6' 5"	6' 1"	Mann's Lures	USA		

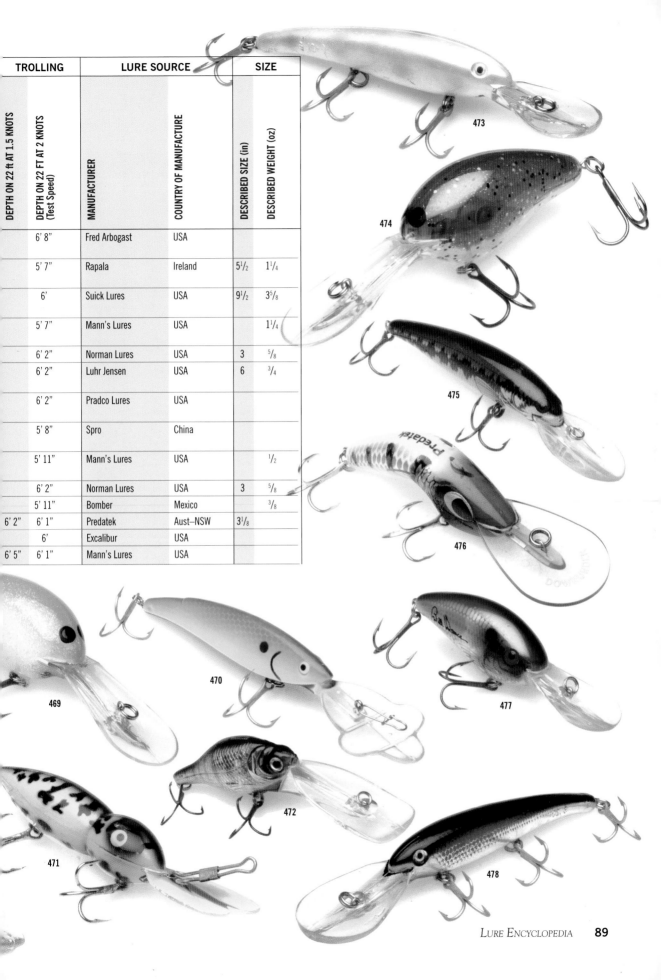

469
470
471
472
473
474
475
476
477
478

NUMBER	LURE	DEPTH (FT) ON 66 FT	MAKER'S STATED DEPTH	ACTION	COMMENTS	FLOATING – SINKING – SUSPENDING	BODY MATERIAL PLASTIC – METAL – WOOD – RUBBER	BIB MATERIAL	WIDTH OF BIB (in)	TOW POINT	ACTUAL WEIGHT (oz)	ACTUAL BODY LENGTH (in)	LENGTH WITH BIB (in)
479	Premier Pro-Model Series 6	19' 9"	15' 9"	Med. sway	Great deep diver		P	Plastic	1.20	Bib	1	$3\frac{1}{8}$	$4\frac{3}{4}$
480	Hot'N Tot Magnum (old)	19' 9"		Med. sway	Great action. Some lateral movement	F	P	Metal	1.31	Bib	$\frac{3}{4}$	3	$4\frac{1}{2}$
481	Stumpjumper 1 deep bib	20'		Med. wide sway	Great action. Must have lure	F	P	Plastic	1.39	Nose	$1\frac{3}{8}$	$4\frac{1}{2}$	$5\frac{7}{8}$
482	Magnum Stretch 18+	20'	18'	Wide sway, medium roll	Better at 2.5 knots. Works well.		P	Plastic	1.73	Bib	$3\frac{7}{8}$	$8\frac{3}{8}$	$10\frac{3}{4}$
483	TD Hyper Crank Ti65	20'		Wide sway	Great action at this speed and slower. Huge rattles.		P	Metal	1.18	Bib	$\frac{5}{8}$	$2\frac{1}{2}$	$4\frac{3}{8}$
484	Lew's Speed Lure Crank	20' 6"		Med. sway, tight roll	Rattle.		P	Plastic	1.25	Bib	$\frac{3}{4}$	3	$4\frac{7}{8}$
485	Suspending Fat Free Shad - Large	20' 9"		Med. wide sway, tight roll	Lunker lure	Sus	P	Plastic	1.31	Bib	$1\frac{1}{8}$	$3\frac{1}{8}$	$4\frac{3}{4}$
486	Magnum CD-26	21'		Med. sway	Needs speed for larger pelagics	S	P	Metal	1.27	Bib	$4\frac{1}{2}$	$10\frac{1}{8}$	$12\frac{1}{2}$
487	Reef Runner Deep Diver	21'	27' 6"	Wide sway	Great action. Lateral movement. Better at 2 knots. One of best lures.		P	Plastic	1.01	Bib	$\frac{5}{8}$	$4\frac{3}{4}$	$6\frac{1}{4}$
488	Hydro Magnum 95 g	21'		Slow med. sway	Great action at 2.5 knots.	S	P	Plastic	1.02	Bib	$3\frac{1}{2}$	7	$9\frac{3}{8}$
489	Hot Lips Express 1/2oz	21' 3"	15'–18'	Med. sway	Classic highly successful		P	Plastic	1.49	Bib	$\frac{5}{8}$	$2\frac{5}{8}$	$4\frac{1}{2}$
490	111MR Deep Diver	21' 6"	25'	Med. sway, tight roll	Hard to get but works well	S	P	Plastic	1.71	Bib	$2\frac{1}{4}$	$6\frac{7}{8}$	$8\frac{5}{8}$

479
480
481
483
484
485

TROLLING		LURE SOURCE		SIZE	
DEPTH ON 22 ft AT 1.5 KNOTS	DEPTH ON 22 FT AT 2 KNOTS (Test Speed)	MANUFACTURER	COUNTRY OF MANUFACTURE	DESCRIBED SIZE (in)	DESCRIBED WEIGHT (oz)
	6'	Strike King Lure Co.	Mexico		
	6' 5"	Storm	USA		
11"	6' 2"	JJ's Lures	Aust–Vic	$3^7/_8$	
	6' 2"	Mann's Lures	USA		
5"	6' 2"	Team Diawa	Japan	$2^1/_2$	$^5/_8$
	6' 5"	Bass Pro Shops	China		
	6' 5"	Excalibur	El Salvador		
	6' 5"	Rapala	Ireland	$10^1/_4$	$4^1/_2$
	6' 6"	Reef Runner Tackle Co.	USA		
	6' 8"	Yo-Zuri Lures	Japan	$7^1/_8$	$3^3/_8$
	6' 6"	Luhr Jensen USA	1/2		
	6' 7"	L&S Lures Mirrolures			

487

488

489

482

490

486

491 492 495 496

NUMBER	LURE	DEPTH		ACTION		LURE PHYSICAL CHARACTERISTICS								
		DEPTH (FT) ON 66 FT	MAKER'S STATED DEPTH	ACTION	COMMENTS	FLOATING – SINKING – SUSPENDING	BODY MATERIAL PLASTIC – METAL – WOOD – RUBBER	BIB MATERIAL	WIDTH OF BIB (in)	TOW POINT	ACTUAL WEIGHT (oz)	ACTUAL BODY LENGTH (in)	LENGTH WITH BIB (in)	
491	Deep Thunder 15	22' 3"	20'–33'	Med. sway, medium roll	Deep…		P	Plastic	1.57	Bib		6	$8^3/_8$	
492	Kadaitcha	22' 6"		Wide sway	Great action. True Australian legend.	F	W	Metal	1.46	Bib	$1^5/_8$	$4^3/_4$	$6^1/_2$	
493	Long A H-Duty	22' 6"		Wide sway	Great action.		P	Plastic	1.25	Bib	$1^1/_2$	6	$8^3/_8$	
494	Magnum CD-18	22' 9"		Med. sway, medium roll	Needs speed	S	W	Metal	1.10	Bib	$2^5/_8$	7	$9^1/_4$	
495	RMG Scorpion 150 XDD Crazy Deep	23'	26' 3"	Wide sway, tight roll	Great action. Better at 2.5 knots.	S	P	Plastic	1.42	Nose	$1^1/_8$	$5^7/_8$	$7^1/_4$	
496	Deep Thunder 15	23' 6"		Med. sway, tight roll	Strong action needs heavy line		P	Plastic	1.57	Bib	2	6	$8^3/_8$	
497	Boomerang Ultra-Deep 80	3' 6"	26' 3"	Med. sway	Better slow. Very deep Australian classic.	F	P	Plastic	1.61	Bib		$3^1/_4$	$5^3/_8$	
498	Heavy Duty Stretch 25+	24'	25'	Med. sway	Needs special gear		P	Plastic	1.61	Bib	$1^3/_4$	$5^7/_8$	8	
499	Magnum CD-22	24' 3"		Med. sway, tight roll	Better at 2.5 knots.	S	P	Metal	1.18	Bib	$3^1/_8$	$8^1/_2$	$10^3/_4$	
500	Hot Lips Express 3/4oz	25'	18'–23'	Wide sway	Great action at both speeds. Still wants to go deeper.		P	Plastic	1.85	Bib	1	$3^1/_4$	$5^3/_8$	
501	Magnum Stretch 30+	26'	30'	Med. sway	Can take really big fish		P	Plastic	2.17	Bib		8	11	
502	Gigantus 50+	27' 6"	50'	Wide sway, wide roll	Limited real applications	S	P	Plastic	3.14	Bib	$13^3/_4$	$11^5/_8$	$15^7/_8$	

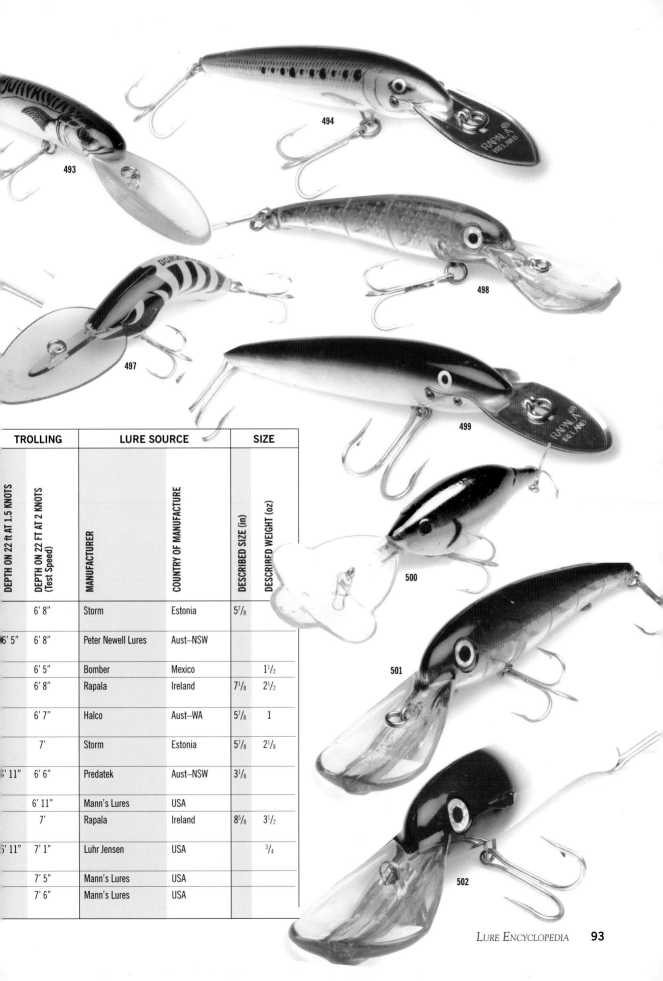

TROLLING		LURE SOURCE		SIZE	
DEPTH ON 22 ft AT 1.5 KNOTS	DEPTH ON 22 FT AT 2 KNOTS (Test Speed)	MANUFACTURER	COUNTRY OF MANUFACTURE	DESCRIBED SIZE (in)	DESCRIBED WEIGHT (oz)
	6' 8"	Storm	Estonia	$5^7/_8$	
6' 5"	6' 8"	Peter Newell Lures	Aust–NSW		
	6' 5"	Bomber	Mexico		$1^1/_2$
	6' 8"	Rapala	Ireland	$7^1/_8$	$2^1/_2$
	6' 7"	Halco	Aust–WA	$5^7/_8$	1
	7'	Storm	Estonia	$5^7/_8$	$2^1/_8$
7' 11"	6' 6"	Predatek	Aust–NSW	$3^1/_8$	
	6' 11"	Mann's Lures	USA		
	7'	Rapala	Ireland	$8^5/_8$	$3^1/_2$
6' 11"	7' 1"	Luhr Jensen	USA		$3/_4$
	7' 5"	Mann's Lures	USA		
	7' 6"	Mann's Lures	USA		

Lure	Manufacturer	No.
Invincible DR8	Nilsmaster	310
Invincible F15	Nilsmaster	364
Invincible Jointed 8	Nilsmaster	196
Jerky Min 100F	River 2 Sea	243
Jigger 3	Nilsmaster	184
Jindivik	Predatek	306
Jitter Mouse 1/8oz	Fred Arbogast	33
Jitterbug 1/4oz	Fred Arbogast	32
Jitterbug 1/8 oz	Fred Arbogast	30
Jitterbug 5/8oz	Fred Arbogast	41
Jitterbug Clicker	Fred Arbogast	36
Jitterbug Clicker 1/4oz	Fred Arbogast	31
Jitterbug JTD 3/8oz	Fred Arbogast	38
Jitterbug JTD 5/8oz	Fred Arbogast	43
Jointed Long A	Bomber	218
Jointed Minnow J-11	Rapala	145
Jointed Minnow J-13	Rapala	299
Jointed Minnow J-5	Rapala	112
Jointed Minnow J-7	Rapala	119
Jointed Minnow J-9	Rapala	163
Jointed Pikie 3000	Creek Chub	339
Jointed Swim Whizz	Homer Le Blanc Tackle	106
Jumbo DD	Nilsmaster	460
Jumpin' Minnow	Rebel	57
Kadaitcha	Peter Newell Lures	492
Kill'r B-I	Bagley	314
Kill'r B-II	Bagley	402
Kill'r B-II Super Shallow	Bagley	127
Klawbaby	Luhr Jensen	214
Klawdad	Luhr Jensen	278
Klawdad	Luhr Jensen	360
Kwikfish K12	Luhr Jensen	357
Kwikfish K15	Luhr Jensen	358
Kwikfish K4	Luhr Jensen	77
Kwikfish K5	Luhr Jensen	92
Kwikfish K7	Luhr Jensen	117
Kwikfish K8	Luhr Jensen	170
Kwikfish K9	Luhr Jensen	69
Laser Pro 120 DD	Halco	321
Laser Pro 120 STD	Halco	219
Laser Pro 160 DD	Halco	365
Laser Pro 160 STD	Halco	200
Laser Pro 190 DD	Halco	386
Laser Pro 190 STD	Halco	179
Laser Pro 45	Halco	187
Lew's Speed Lure Crank	Bass Pro Shops	484
Lightning Minnow #1	The Producers	168
Lightning Minnow #2	The Producers	408
Little Tasmanian Devil	Wigston's	64
Little Z	The Producers	295
Long A	Bomber	475
Long A 3/8oz	Bomber	217
Long A H-Duty	Bomber	493
Long A H-Duty 7/8oz	Bomber	239
Long A Magnum 1 1/2oz	Bomber	241
Long A Minnow	Bomber	428
Long A Minnow 1/2oz	Bomber	208

Lure	Manufacturer	No.
Long A Select Series	Bomber	222
Long Cast Minnow LC12	Rapala	172
Lucky 13	Heddon	15
Mad N	Norman Lures	260
Magnum CD-11	Rapala	409
Magnum CD-14	Rapala	466
Magnum CD-18	Rapala	494
Magnum CD-22	Rapala	499
Magnum CD-26	Rapala	486
Magnum CD-7	Rapala	331
Magnum CD-9	Rapala	443
Magnum Mag-11	Rapala	298
Magnum Mag-14	Rapala	372
Magnum Mag-18	Rapala	366
Magnum Mag-7	Rapala	202
Magnum Mag-9	Rapala	204
Magnum Stretch 18+	Mann's Lures	482
Magnum Stretch 30+	Mann's Lures	501
Magnum Stretch 8+	Mann's Lures	340
Magnum wiggle wart (USA made)	Storm	418
Master Shad	Bagley	195
Mega Ghost	The Producers	58
MicroMin - Deep	Predatek	296
MicroMin - Shallow	Predatek	230
Mid Wart	Storm	313
Midi S	Shakespeare Lures	328
Midive Min 140S	River 2 Sea	395
Midive Min 80F	River 2 Sea	270
Mimic Series 80	Saiko Lures	320
Mini Fat Rap	Rapala	167
Mini Whacker 1/6oz	Bomber	76
Mini Z Shallow	The Producers	225
Mini-Me Ghost F	The Producers	50
MinMin Deep	Predatek	289
MinMin Shallow	Predatek	182
Minnow Spin Super Vibrax 1	Blue Fox	104
Minnow Spin Super Vibrax 2	Blue Fox	78
Mirashad Fry Size MS50SP	Owner Lures	216
MMLS Crankbait	L&S Lures Mirrolures	135
Model 2A	Bomber	284
Model 5A	Bomber	330
Model 6A	Bomber	414
Model 7A	Bomber	435
Mohican Dart	Dream Catcher Lures	326
Monster Popper F	The Producers	45
Moonsault CB-350	Lucky Craft Lures	447
Mud Bug	Fred Arbogast	465
Mud Bug 1/4oz	Fred Arbogast	342
Mud Bug 1/8oz	Fred Arbogast	324
Mud Bug 5/8oz	Fred Arbogast	397
Mystic Ghost Minnow	Rebel	108
Nature Hopper 1/8oz	Blue Fox	89
Night Walker	Halco	40
Obese Crank 45	River 2 Sea	293
Original Minnow 11	Rapala	183
Original Minnow 13	Rapala	146
Original Minnow 18	Rapala	291

Lure	Manufacturer	No.
Original Minnow 3	Rapala	129
Original Minnow 5	Rapala	137
Original Minnow 7	Rapala	153
Original Minnow 9	Rapala	152
Oxboro Ox Spoon	Oxboro Outdoors	79
Pencil Popper Large	Cotton Cordell	49
Pencil Popper Small	Cotton Cordell	48
Piglet	Odyssey Lures	242
Pin's Minnow	Yo-Zuri Lures	111
Poltergeist 50	Halco	379
Popper 5/8oz F	The Producers	6
Pop-R Excalibur	Rebel	9
Power Dive Minnow	Luhr Jensen	470
Power Dive Minnow 1/2oz	Luhr Jensen	455
Power Minnow	Luhr Jensen	246
Power Minnow	Luhr Jensen	367
Power Minnow Suspending	Luhr Jensen	346
Premier Pro-Model Series 1	Strike King Lure Company	282
Premier Pro-Model Series 4S	Strike King Lure Company	308
Premier Pro-Model Series 5	Strike King Lure Company	434
Premier Pro-Model Series 6	Strike King Lure Company	479
Prime DD Crankbait 25	Spro	472
Prism Shad	The Producers	256
Prism Shad #3S	The Producers	323
Pro Long 15A	Bomber	251
Probe	Rabble Rouser Lures	424
Pro's Choice Lil Lonnie	Stanley Jigs	411
Pro's Choice Minnow	Stanley Jigs	134
Prospector 3"	Possum Lures	240
Rat-L-Trap Magnum Force	Bill Lewis Lures	355
Rat-L-Trap Magnum Trap	Bill Lewis Lures	373
Rat-L-Trap Mini Trap	Bill Lewis Lures	227
Rat-L-Trap Rattletrap	Bill Lewis Lures	301
Rat-L-Trap Tiny Trap	Bill Lewis Lures	194
Rattlin' Chug Bug	Storm	14
Rattlin' Fat Rap RFR-5	Rapala	361
Rattlin' Fat Rap RFR-7	Rapala	383
Rattlin' Rapala RNR-4	Rapala	174
Rattlin' Rapala RNR5	Rapala	213
Rattlin' Rapala RNR7	Rapala	303
Rattlin' Rapala RNR8	Rapala	316
Rattlin' Rogue ARB1200	Smithwick	192
Rattlin' Rogue ASSRB1200	Smithwick	456
Reef Runner Deep Diver	Reef Runner Tackle Co	487
Risto Rap RR-8	Rapala	448
River Minnow	The Producers	288
RMG Poltergeist 80	Halco	450
RMG Rellik Doc	Halco	348
RMG Scorpion 125 DD	Halco	385
RMG Scorpion 125 SR	Halco	245
RMG Scorpion 125 STD	Halco	345
RMG Scorpion 150 DD	Halco	464
RMG Scorpion 150 STD	Halco	399
RMG Scorpion 150 XDD	Halco	495
RMG Scorpion 35 STD	Halco	161

Lure	Manufacturer	No.
RMG Scorpion 52 DD	Halco	279
RMG Scorpion 52 STD	Halco	277
RMG Scorpion 68 DD	Halco	329
RMG Scorpion 68 STD	Halco	305
RMG Scorpion 90 DD	Halco	420
RMG Scorpion 90 STD	Halco	359
RMG Sneaky Bream Scorpion 35	Halco	159
Rooster Tail 1/6oz	Worden's	98
Rooster Tail 1/8oz	Worden's	81
Roscoe's Shiner 4	The Producers	148
Roscoe's Shiner 5	The Producers	121
Roscoe's Shiner 7	The Producers	211
Saltwater Chug Bug	Storm	46
Saltwater Chug Bug 8 cm	Storm	13
Saltwater Thunderstick	Storm	238
Salty Tasmanian Devil 40 g	Wigston's	110
Salty Tasmanian Devil 70 g	Wigston's	166
Scale Raza 20+	DK Lures	444
Sea Min 120 F	River 2 Sea	255
Shad Rap Suspending RS5	Rapala	412
Shad Rap Deep SR5	Rapala	307
Shad Rap Deep SR7	Rapala	374
Shad Rap Deep SR8	Rapala	376
Shad Rap Deep SR9	Rapala	449
Shad Rap Jointed JSR4	Rapala	205
Shad Rap Jointed JSR5	Rapala	350
Shad Rap Shallow 5	Rapala	186
Shad Rap Shallow 7	Rapala	175
Shad Rap Shallow 8	Rapala	215
Shad Rap Shallow 9	Rapala	261
Shad Rap Suspending RS7	Rapala	446
Shakespeare Minnow	Shakespeare Lures	235
Shallow A	Bomber	122
Shallow Sand Viper	Predatek	210
Shallow Thunder 11	Storm	162
Shallow Thunder 15	Storm	221
Shallow Thunder 15	Storm	223
Skitter Pop SP-5	Rapala	7
Skitter Pop SP-7	Rapala	12
Skitter Pop SP-9	Rapala	16
Skitter Pop SSP-12	Rapala	47
Skitter Prop SPR-7	Rapala	25
Slap-Stick	Bill Lewis Lures	180
Slavko Bug	Yo-Zuri Lures	309
Sliver Jointed 13	Rapala	335
Sliver Jointed 20	Rapala	442
Small Fry Bass	Bagley	247
Small Fry Crayfish	Bagley	286
Snap Shad super small	Yo-Zuri Lures	133
Spearhead 8	Nilsmaster	264
Spence Scout	Strike King Lure Company	266
Spit'n Image	Excalibur	52
Spit'n Image Jr	Excalibur	51
Spoonbill	Predatek	445
Spoonbill Super Rogue	Smithwick	371
Sputterbuzz	Fred Arbogast	20

Lure	Manufacturer	No.
Stalwart 8	Nilsmaster	253
Stanley Minnow	Stanley Jigs	220
Static Shad 60 Su	River 2 Sea	333
Static Shad 70 Su	River 2 Sea	287
Streaker 10 g	Halco	68
Streaker 20 g	Halco	83
Streaker 30 g	Halco	88
Streaker 40 g	Halco	87
Stretch 1 Minus	Mann's Lures	132
Stretch 10+	Mann's Lures	433
Stretch 20+	Mann's Lures	478
Stretch 5+	Mann's Lures	315
Stumpjumper 1 deep bib	JJ's Lures	481
Stumpjumper 1 shallow bib	JJ's Lures	375
Stumpjumper 2 deep bib	JJ's Lures	415
Stumpjumper 2 round bib	JJ's Lures	401
Stumpjumper 2 shallow bib	JJ's Lures	387
Stumpjumper 3 deep straight bib	JJ's Lures	351
Stumpjumper 3 shallow bib	JJ's Lures	249
Sub Wart	Storm	113
Sub Wart 5 cm	Storm	102
Super Shad Rap 14	Rapala	352
Super Spot	Cotton Cordell	271
Super Spot	Cotton Cordell	274
Super Spot	Cotton Cordell	193
Super Vibrax 0	Blue Fox	75
Super Vibrax 1	Blue Fox	82
Super Vibrax 2	Blue Fox	97
Super Vibrax 3	Blue Fox	109
Super Vibrax 4	Blue Fox	99
Super Vibrax 5	Blue Fox	115
Super Vibrax 6	Blue Fox	103
Super Vibrax Minnow Spin 2	Blue Fox	85
Surfi Vib 80	River 2 Sea	267
Suspend DD-22	Norman Lures	469
Suspending Fat Free Fry	Excalibur	451
Suspending Fat Free Shad	Excalibur	477
Suspending Fat Free Shad - Large	Excalibur	485
Suspending Super Rogue	Smithwick	272
Suspending Thunder Stick	Storm	252
Swim'n Image Shallow Runner	Excalibur	203
Tadpolly	Heddon	317
Tail Dancer TD7	Rapala	281
Tail Dancer TD9	Rapala	334
Tasmanian Devil 13.5 g	Wigston's	86
Tasmanian Devil 7 g	Wigston's	67
Tasmanian Devil Dual Depth	Wigston's	147
Tasmanian Devil Dual Depth Deep	Wigston's	165
TD Hyper Crank	Team Diawa	363
TD Hyper Crank Ti65	Team Diawa	483
TD Hyper Minnow	Team Diawa	140
TD Hyper Minnow	Team Diawa	142
TD Hyper Minnow 90	Team Diawa	300
TD Hyper Shad Ti60	Team Diawa	297

Lure	Manufacturer	No.
Team Esko TE7	Rapala	171
Teeny Crawfish	Rebel	149
Teeny Pop R	Rebel	5
Teeny Torpedo	Heddon	17
Teeny Wee Frog	Rebel	107
The Original Pig	Odyssey Lures	209
Thunder Crank	Storm	457
Thunder Crank 6	Storm	368
Thunder Dog	Storm	56
Thunderstick	Storm	236
Thunderstick 11	Storm	237
Thunderstick 6	Storm	189
Tilsan Barra	Halco	391
Tilsan Bass	Halco	429
Tilsan Minnow	Halco	343
Tiny Crazy Crawler	Heddon	34
Tiny N	Norman Lures	201
Tiny Torpedo	Heddon	18
Trembler 110	Halco	341
Trembler 70	Halco	275
Triho Min 120F	River 2 Sea	206
Triho Min 180F	River 2 Sea	349
Tru Track Classic	Andreas Tackle	93
Tru Track Classic 1 oz	Andreas Tackle	169
Tru Track Pro 3/4 oz	Andreas Tackle	128
Tru Track Spin 1/2 oz	Andreas Tackle	143
Tumbleweed Charlie's Spinnerbait 3/8oz	The Producers	118
Turbo #1	The Producers	19
Turbo #2	The Producers	23
Twisty 15 g	Halco	74
Twisty 20 g	Halco	95
Twisty 5 g	Halco	60
Twisty 55 g	Halco	158
Vibrax Minnow Chaser 1	Blue Fox	123
Vibrax Minnow Chaser 2	Blue Fox	105
Viper 150	Predatek	431
Wally Minnow CS8	Cotton Cordell	463
Wee Crawfish	Rebel	231
Wee Frog	Rebel	176
Wiggle 'O'	Cotton Cordell	430
Wiggle Wart	Storm	381
Wiggle Wart	Storm	427
Willy's Worm No 1	The Producers	356
Willy's Worm No 2	The Producers	389
Willy's Worm No 3	The Producers	390
Wobbler 10 g Sparkler	Halco	66
Wobbler 20 g Sparkler	Halco	61
Wobbler 30 g Sparkler	Halco	71
Wobbler 40 g Sparkler	Halco	70
Woodchopper	Luhr Jensen	28
Woodchopper 1/2oz	Luhr Jensen	24
Woodchopper 3/8oz	Luhr Jensen	22
Woomera	Predatek	369
X 4 Flatfish	Worden's	259
XL Jitterbug	Fred Arbogast	44
Zero #2	The Producers	212
Zero #3	The Producers	302